DAILY WRITING WARM-UPS

Written by
Trisha Callella

Editor: Stacey Faulkner
Illustrator: Darcy Tom
Designer: Moonhee Pak
Art Director: Tom Cochrane
Project Director: Sue Lewis

Table of Contents

Introduction

Daily Writing Warm-ups provides teachers and students with the tools necessary to make writing improvement easy. Use this resource to reinforce writing skills and show children how to apply that information to enhance their own writing performance. The skills and strategies in this book are presented in a systematic format and provide means for direct application. Plan for students to complete the reproducibles in the order that they appear so that the students can benefit from the spiraling scope and sequence. This resource provides a warm-up for almost every day of the school year!

Each Writing Warm-up has the same format in order to help you quickly identify areas of need and success. For example, if a student consistently makes errors on #3 on every page, you immediately know that the student needs more help with vocabulary development.

FORMAT FOR EVERY WRITING WARM-UP	
Number	**Objective**
1	Parts of Speech
2	Editing (spelling and mechanics)
3	Enriched Vocabulary
4	Revising (word choice and verb tense)
5	Organization
6	Content
Quickwrite	Application of All Skills

NATIONAL STANDARDS

Daily Writing Warm-ups helps you reinforce standards set by the National Council of Teachers of English at the beginning of every single writing lesson, every single day. It will also give students the opportunity to do the following:

- Apply knowledge of language structure and conventions of print to convey ideas effectively.
- Use written language to communicate to a variety of audiences and for different purposes.
- Accomplish their own purpose through written language.

SPECIAL FEATURES

The format for *Daily Writing Warm-ups* is simple, yet the organization is highly structured.

The following additional features are included in this resource:

- Standards-based skills are scaffolded from one Writing Warm-up to another. Each lesson builds upon prior learning.
- The order of the questions leads from skills to strategies. For example, students will practice using proper mechanics (e.g., punctuation) in the editing exercise before moving on to the revising exercise in which students practice word choice and sentence structure.
- The quizzes are structured and build on one another throughout the book.
- A variety of writing purposes are included (e.g., narrative, descriptive, compare/contrast).
- Each Writing Warm-up is created around a topic to help provide background knowledge necessary for successful writing.
- Students document their progress by skill categories that are listed in the Scope and Sequence (pages 6–7).
- Both standardized test formats and open-ended questions are provided to reach and teach every learner.

FACTORS FOR STUDENT SUCCESS

The key factors for student success are daily practice, strategic teaching at teachable moments, and opportunities to share ideas and answers during grading. Enjoy using this book! You will know that you are providing explicit, systematic writing instruction on a daily basis.

Getting Started

WARMING UP

For each student, photocopy the Writing Warm-ups and Quickwrite form (page 9) in advance and bind them together in a three-ring binder. Photocopy and bind one section at a time. Remember to photocopy the quizzes separately, and set those aside for use as needed.

Every day, begin the writing session by having students take out their binder. Refer to the Scope and Sequence on pages 6–7, and discuss with students the objectives of that day's Writing Warm-ups sheet. Then let them begin the warm-up for that day. When the class is finished, review the answers and expand on any teachable moments that arise.

Writing Warm-up	Parts of Speech 1	Editing 2	Enriched Vocabulary 3	Revising 4
1–9	nouns	spelling, capitals & ending punctuation	identify synonyms & antonyms	apply word usage & enriched vocabulary
10–18	verbs	all of the above & contractions	identify synonyms & antonyms	apply word usage & enriched vocabulary
19–27	nouns & verbs	all of the above & commas in a list	identify synonyms & antonyms	all of the above & match tenses
28–36	pronouns	all of the above & homophones	identify synonyms & antonyms	all of the above & pronoun match
37–45	nouns & pronouns	review all of the above & homophones	identify synonyms & antonyms	all of the above & pronoun match

ABOUT THE QUICKWRITES

At the end of each Writing Warm-up page, there is a short writing prompt designed to provide direct application of the skills and strategies in authentic writing. Stress the importance of the Quickwrites so that students understand the necessity for reinforcing the skills they have practiced.

QUIZZES AND GRADING

At the completion of every nine warm-up sheets, administer the appropriate quiz. Record that grade in your grade book. Because of time constraints, it may not be possible to grade every Quickwrite, so periodically ask students to turn one in. Grade their papers and return them promptly. Refer to the Quickwrite Rubric on page 10 for assistance in scoring student writing.

KEEPING TRACK OF PROGRESS

Have students keep track of their own progress once they are familiar with the structure and routine of the warm-ups. Give them a copy of the Progress Record (page 8) to encourage students to take on the responsibility and ownership of their learning. Have students put a checkmark in the appropriate box for each incorrect item and a score for each Quickwrite that is graded. Collect the form every two weeks to monitor whether or not students are mastering the objectives. Refer to the Scope and Sequence to plan accordingly when reteaching a skill is necessary.

Scope and Sequence

Writing Warm-up	Parts of Speech 1	Editing 2	Enriched Vocabulary 3	Revising 4
1–9	nouns	spelling, capitals & ending punctuation	identify synonyms & antonyms	apply word usage & enriched vocabulary
10–18	verbs	all of the above & contractions	identify synonyms & antonyms	apply word usage & enriched vocabulary
19–27	nouns & verbs	all of the above & commas in a list	identify synonyms & antonyms	all of the above & match tenses
28–36	pronouns	all of the above & homophones	identify synonyms & antonyms	all of the above & pronoun match
37–45	nouns & pronouns	review all of the above & homophones	identify synonyms & antonyms	all of the above & pronoun match
46–54	adjectives	review all of the above	identify synonyms & antonyms	review all of the above
55–63	nouns & adjectives	review all of the above	write three synonyms	review all of the above
64–72	adverbs	review all of the above	write three synonyms	review all of the above
73–81	conjunctions	review all of the above & comma before conjunctions	write one synonym & one antonym	review all of the above & enriched vocabulary
82–90	prepositions	review all of the above	good vs. well	review all of the above & write correct conjunction
91–99	review all of the above	review all of the above	bad vs. badly less vs. fewer	review all of the above

Daily Writing Warm-ups 3–4 © 2006 Creative Teaching Press

Scope and Sequence

Writing Warm-up	Organization 5	Content 6	Quickwrite
1–9	identify best topic sentence	identify problem with the paragraph	All About Me
10–18	identify best topic sentence	identify problem with the paragraph	If Given the Chance
19–27	identify best concluding sentence	identify problem with the paragraph	Yum! Yum!
28–36	identify best concluding sentence	identify problem with the paragraph	Never Say Never
37–45	identify sentence out of sequence	identify detail that does not support topic sentence	Give Me Five!
46–54	identify sentence out of sequence	identify detail that best supports topic sentence	This or That?
55–63	identify best sentence sequence	identify sentence that shows giving own advice	Advice Column
64–72	identify best sentence sequence	identify specific point of view	A Day in the Life
73–81	identify sentences to combine with conjunction	identify sentence not relevant to the topic	Thinking of Others
82–90	identify best use of enriched vocabulary	identify sentence with the most positive tone	So Many Similes
91–99	write a topic sentence	identify biggest content problem	Interpreter Needed!

_____'s Progress Record

	NUMBERED ITEM						
WRITING WARM-UP #	Parts of Speech 1	Editing 2	Enriched Vocabulary 3	Revising 4	Organization 5	Content 6	Quickwrite

Daily Writing Warm-ups 3–4 © 2006 Creative Teaching Press

QUICKWRITE

Topic _____

_____

_____

_____

_____

_____

_____

_____

_____

_____

_____

_____

_____

_____

_____

QUICKWRITE RUBRIC

Objective	Criteria				Value
	1	**2**	**3**	**4**	
Parts of Speech	many parts of speech were misused	some parts of speech were misused	few parts of speech were misused	no parts of speech were misused	_____
Mechanics	many errors with spelling, capitalization, and punctuation	some errors with spelling, capitalization, and punctuation	few errors with spelling, capitalization, and punctuation	no errors with spelling, capitalization, or punctuation	_____
Enriched Vocabulary	writing contains slang and many basic words	writing contains some basic words such as *good* and *nice*	writing contains several descriptive words	writing contains rich, descriptive vocabulary	_____
Sentence Structure	no sentence variation; short, choppy sentences; many run-ons or fragments; mixed tenses throughout	some sentence variation, some simple sentences should be combined, 1–2 run-ons or fragments, tenses change 1–2 times	variety of sentence starters, complex sentences used, all sentences are complete, tenses used are consistent	creative variety of sentence starters, advanced sentence structure (colons, semicolons), consistent use of tenses contribute to clarity/style	_____
Organization	no sequence, ideas jump around, topic or concluding sentence missing, no use of details	sequence shows some sense of logic, topic or concluding sentence is not related to main idea, limited use of details	sequence is logical, topic and concluding sentence relate to main idea, details support topic	effective sequencing enhances writing, topic sentence is inviting, concluding sentence demonstrates closure, thoughtful placement of quality details	_____
Content	drifted off topic many times, majority of information is irrelevant, written for wrong audience	drifted off topic 1–2 times, 1–2 pieces of irrelevant information, voice shifts between different audiences	stayed on topic, all information is relevant, correct voice for intended audience	all parts of topic are addressed, relevant information demonstrates insight or goes beyond the obvious, voice enhanced the writing	_____

Daily Writing Warm-ups 3–4 © 2006 Creative Teaching Press

Name_____   Date _____

Writing Warm-up 1

1 Underline the nouns in the sentence below.
She woke up, made her bed, and then brushed her teeth.

2 Edit the following sentence, and rewrite it on the line below.
did you remember to hang your towel on the bar

_____

3 Which word is **not** a synonym for *large*?
Ⓐ enormous   Ⓑ massive   Ⓒ gigantic   Ⓓ tiny

4 Revise the sentence below.
She packed a large lunch, but she didn't eat one biting at school.

_____

5 Choose the best topic sentence for the paragraph.
_____ **I can already write funny stories. Many people are also surprised to see how well I can throw a football. Perhaps they are surprised because I'm only eight years old. In a short time, I have accomplished many things.**
Ⓐ I am good at many things.
Ⓑ Sometimes I surprise people by what I can already do.
Ⓒ Even though I'm young, I am very smart.
Ⓓ One should never underestimate what a child can do.

6 What is wrong with the paragraph in number 5?
Ⓐ most sentences start the same
Ⓑ too many simple words should have been changed using synonyms
Ⓒ the sentences are all too short and choppy
Ⓓ none of the above

PREWRITE On the back of this paper, draw six boxes with arrows pointing from one box to the next. Inside the boxes, write the first six things you do every morning in order.

QUICKWRITE Describe your typical morning routine before arriving at school. Use the sequence of events you listed on the back to get started.

Name_____   Date _____

Writing Warm-up 2

1 Underline the nouns in the sentence below.
My favorite character in the book was funny, generous, and honest.

2 Edit the following sentence, and rewrite it on the line below.
i remember the title, but what was that story abowt

_____

3 Which word is **not** a synoynm for _nice_?
    Ⓐ likable   Ⓑ friendly   Ⓒ cordial   Ⓓ funny

4 Revise the sentence below.
My little sister is not nice to me, because sometimes she bits me to get her way.

_____

5 Choose the best topic sentence for the paragraph.
_____ **Some people are honest. Some people are trustworthy. Some people are generous with their time and money. Some people can be described as having positive personality traits.**
    Ⓐ Honesty is an important personality trait.
    Ⓑ People like to spend time around others who are trustworthy.
    Ⓒ Intelligence is not a personality trait.
    Ⓓ Personality traits describe a person's overall character and behavior.

6 What is wrong with the paragraph in number 5?
    Ⓐ most sentences start the same
    Ⓑ too many simple words should
        have been changed using synonyms
    Ⓒ the sentences are all too short
        and choppy
    Ⓓ none of the above

PREWRITE
On the back of this paper, draw three boxes. Label each box with a positive personality trait that describes you.

QUICKWRITE
Look at the three traits that you listed. Write a paragraph describing your three best personality traits. Include a specific example for each trait.

Writing Warm-up 3

1 Underline the nouns in the sentence below.
   Would you like to come over to my house to meet my family?

2 Edit the following sentence, and rewrite it on the line below.
   can you name everie member of your family

_____

3 Which word or phrase is **not** a synonym for _loving_?
   Ⓐ cruel   Ⓑ devoted   Ⓒ caring   Ⓓ warm-hearted

4 Revise the sentence below.
   All of the members in Dave's loving family growed up sharing one small apartment.

_____

5 Choose the best topic sentence for the paragraph.
   _____ **Once I needed help. I fell and scraped my knee. My sister came to the rescue. She cleaned and bandaged my cut. I was lucky. The people in my family have always been there for me.**
   Ⓐ My family will always be there to lend me a hand.
   Ⓑ It is not fun getting hurt.
   Ⓒ Everyone has a family.
   Ⓓ You should be thankful for your family.

6 What is wrong with the paragraph in number 5?
   Ⓐ most sentences start the same
   Ⓑ too many simple words should have been changed using synonyms
   Ⓒ the sentences are all too short and choppy
   Ⓓ none of the above

PREWRITE On the back of this paper, draw three boxes. Label each box with the name of a family member. Below each name, list three words that describe that person.

QUICKWRITE Look at your list of three family members and their characteristics. Why are they important to you? Describe one way each person has been there for you in a time of need.

Name_____ Date _____

Writing Warm-up 4

1 Underline the nouns in the sentence below.
A talent is a natural ability for doing something well.

2 Edit the following sentence, and rewrite it on the line below.
i no how to do a cartwheel and a back flip

_____

3 Which word is **not** a synonym for _hard_ as in _"hard_ work"?
    Ⓐ difficult   Ⓑ challenging   Ⓒ simple   Ⓓ tough

4 Revise the sentence below.
Practicing every day was hard, but it helped Jill's knowledge of swimming techniques growed over time.

_____

5 Choose the best topic sentence for the paragraph.
_____ **Some people are beautiful singers. Others are good at solving math problems. Creating new inventions is considered a talent. It may take some time to discover, but everyone has a talent.**
    Ⓐ Talents require practice.
    Ⓑ My biggest talent is writing books.
    Ⓒ Everyone has some type of talent.
    Ⓓ Some people are talented in the area of music.

6 What is wrong with the paragraph in number 5?
    Ⓐ most sentences start the same
    Ⓑ too many simple words should have been changed using synonyms
    Ⓒ the sentences are all too short and choppy
    Ⓓ none of the above

PREWRITE On the back of this paper, draw six boxes. Label each box with something you do well. If your ability could be considered a talent, then draw a star above the box.

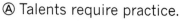

QUICKWRITE Look at the boxes you labeled with a star. Describe your talents. How might they be useful or helpful in your future?

Writing Warm-up 5

1 Underline the nouns in the sentence below.
A pet peeve is something that simply drives you crazy whenever you see it happening.

2 Edit the following sentence, and rewrite it on the line below.
did you see how often he chewed with his mouth open at tonite's dinner

_____

3 Which word is **not** a synonym for *looking* as in "*looking* at her watch while the teacher spoke"?
Ⓐ glancing   Ⓑ peeking   Ⓒ staring   Ⓓ peeping

4 Revise the sentence below.
His pet peeve is when his daughter says, "That's all I get?" when he buyed her something.

_____

5 Choose the best topic sentence for the paragraph.
_____ **My list begins with people who don't say "thank you" when receiving a gift. Another pet peeve of mine is people who do not look at me when I'm speaking. My ultimate pet peeve is people who say they will do something and then forget. These are just a few of my pet peeves.**
Ⓐ If you have a pet peeve, then you should tell that person.
Ⓑ Most people can think of pet peeves that annoy them.
Ⓒ A pet peeve is different from a bad habit.
Ⓓ To some people, being late to an appointment is a pet peeve.

6 What is wrong with the paragraph in number 5?
Ⓐ most sentences start the same
Ⓑ too many simple words should have been changed using synonyms
Ⓒ the sentences are all too short and choppy
Ⓓ none of the above

Thank you!

PREWRITE Turn this paper over, and draw a vertical line and a horizontal line dividing your paper into four boxes. In each box, write something that drives you crazy.

QUICKWRITE Look at your pet peeves. Describe them in clear detail. Be sure to include reasons why they drive you crazy.

Daily Writing Warm-ups 3–4 © 2006 Creative Teaching Press

Writing Warm-up 6

1 Underline the nouns in the sentence below.
My best subjects in school are reading, writing, and math.

2 Edit the following sentence, and rewrite it on the line below.
in skool, math seems to be my best subject every year

_____

3 Which word is **not** a synonym for _smart_?
Ⓐ intelligent   Ⓑ popular   © clever   Ⓓ brainy

4 Revise the sentence below.
I think I'm good when it comes to solving math problems because I do them in my head.

_____

5 Choose the best topic sentence for the paragraph.
_____ **I am good at reading. I understand what I read. Books are fun to read. My reading scores are high. Reading is my best subject.**
Ⓐ Few people are strong students at every subject in school.
Ⓑ I am intelligent in many different school subjects.
© Reading is easy for me.
Ⓓ Even though someone finds a subject easy,
   it is still important to study and do homework.

6 What is wrong with the paragraph in number 5?
Ⓐ most sentences start the same
Ⓑ too many simple words should have been changed using synonyms
© the sentences are all too short and choppy
Ⓓ none of the above

PREWRITE Turn this paper over, and draw a line dividing your paper in half. On one side, list the subject you find the easiest. On the other side, list the subject you find the most difficult.

QUICKWRITE Which subject is the easiest for you? Why? Which subject is the hardest for you? Why?

Daily Writing Warm-ups 3–4 © 2006 Creative Teaching Press

Writing Warm-up 7

1 Underline the nouns in the sentence below.
On weekends, many children enjoy watching cartoons in the morning before going outside to play with friends.

2 Edit the following sentence, and rewrite it on the line below.
it's allmost time for you to go to bed now

_____

3 Which word is **not** a synonym for *fun* as in "*fun* weekend plans"?
Ⓐ exciting   Ⓑ enjoyable   Ⓒ annoying   Ⓓ entertaining

4 Revise the sentence below.
We have fun activities planned for the weekend including builds my new bed and paint the walls.

_____

5 Choose the best topic sentence for the paragraph.
_____ **We wake up later than we do on school days. After we wake up, we usually relax by the television. Later, we'll play games together. It doesn't matter what we do, as long as we are enjoying time together.**
Ⓐ It's important to rest, relax, and spend time with family on weekends.
Ⓑ Weekends are great, because we can sleep in late.
Ⓒ On weekends, my family likes to go to the park.
Ⓓ Weekends give my family a chance to spend time together.

6 What is wrong with the paragraph in number 5?
Ⓐ most sentences start the same
Ⓑ too many simple words should have been changed using synonyms
Ⓒ the sentences are all too short and choppy
Ⓓ none of the above

PREWRITE
Turn this paper over, and draw four large boxes. In each box, write one thing you do almost every weekend. Below each activity, list three words or phrases that describe it.

QUICKWRITE
What do you enjoy doing on weekends? How is that different from the weekdays?

Name_____   Date _____

Writing Warm-up 8

1 Underline the nouns in the sentence below.
Her dad reads her a story every night before she goes to bed.

2 Edit the following sentence, and rewrite it on the line below.
she wanted to stay up an hour later becus her favorite show was delayed

_____

3 Which word is **not** a synonym for *sweet* as in *"sweet dreams"*?
    Ⓐ sugary   Ⓑ pleasant   Ⓒ happy   Ⓓ peaceful

4 Revise the sentence below.
After she tucked her son in bed, she began built a triple-layer cake for his party.

_____

5 Choose the best topic sentence for the paragraph.
_____ **First, I brush my teeth. Next, I comb my hair. Then, I put on my pajamas. After that, I kiss my family good night. Then I listen to a story. Finally, I fall asleep.**
    Ⓐ It was a great night.
    Ⓑ Each night I do the same thing.
    Ⓒ Some people do things in a certain order each night.
    Ⓓ My friends and I do the same things before going to bed each night.

6 What is wrong with the paragraph in number 5?
    Ⓐ most sentences start the same
    Ⓑ too many simple words should have been changed using synonyms
    Ⓒ the sentences are all too short and choppy
    Ⓓ none of the above

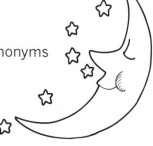

PREWRITE Turn this paper over, and draw five boxes with arrows pointing from one box to the next. Inside the boxes, list in order five things you do every night before you fall asleep.

QUICKWRITE Look at your list of nightly activities. Describe your typical evening routine.

Daily Writing Warm-ups 3–4 © 2006 Creative Teaching Press

Writing Warm-up 9

1   Underline the nouns in the sentence below.
    Many students often do their homework without being asked.

2   Edit the following sentence, and rewrite it on the line below.
    did you no that doing your homework is one way to become an even better student

_____

3   Which word or phrase is **not** a synonym for *try*?
    Ⓐ abandon   Ⓑ attempt   Ⓒ apply effort   Ⓓ aim

4   Revise the sentence below.
    His goal was to improve his grades, so he hitted the books and tried studying harder.

_____

5   Choose the best topic sentence for the paragraph.
    _____ **One way is to focus on the learning rather than on what your friends are doing. One way is to study for a longer time. One way is to do your homework before playing. These are just a few ways you can become a better student.**
    Ⓐ The best students get into the best colleges.
    Ⓑ One way to be a better student is to take notes in class.
    Ⓒ There are many ways you can become a better student.
    Ⓓ Being a strong student will help you to have a better future.

6   What is wrong with the paragraph in number 5?
    Ⓐ most sentences start the same
    Ⓑ too many simple words should have been changed using synonyms
    Ⓒ the sentences are all too short and choppy
    Ⓓ none of the above

 **PREWRITE** Turn this paper over, and draw a vertical line and a horizontal line dividing your paper into four boxes. In each box, name one of your strengths as a student.

 **QUICKWRITE** What are your strengths as a student? What can you do to become an even better student?

QUIZ 1

1 Underline any nouns in the sentence below.
I have a dog, two cats, and six rabbits at my house.

2 Edit the following sentence, and rewrite it on the line below.
i'm going to the doctor agin, becus i can't get rid of my sore throat

_____

3 Which word is **not** a synonym for *fun* as in "a *fun* classroom"?
Ⓐ adorable
Ⓑ entertaining
Ⓒ exciting
Ⓓ enjoyable

4 Revise the sentence below.
When the number of children in her family hitted five, Mrs. Brown realized she had outgrowed her house.

_____

_____

5 Write a topic sentence for the paragraph.

_____

Jenny's mom had outlined some exciting vacation plans. First, they would fly to Hawaii. After landing, they would visit their hotel room just long enough to drop off their luggage. Then they would head to the beach to try surfing in the clear waters of the island. They couldn't wait to leave on their first family vacation.

6 What is wrong with the paragraph in number 5?
Ⓐ most sentences start the same
Ⓑ too many simple words should have been changed using synonyms
Ⓒ the sentences are all too short and choppy
Ⓓ none of the above

Give your best effort!

SCORE

Daily Writing Warm-ups 3–4 © 2006 Creative Teaching Press

Name_____ Date _____

Writing Warm-up 10

1 Underline the verbs in the sentence below.
The president of the United States is elected by the citizens every four years.

2 Edit the following sentence, and rewrite it on the line below.
have you heard about the air force one exhibit at the presidential library

_____

3 Which word is **not** a synonym for *help* as in "the president will *help*"?
    Ⓐ assist   Ⓑ support   Ⓒ hinder   Ⓓ aid

4 Revise the sentence below.
They are trying to built a new set of laws to help the president boost the economy.

_____

5 Choose the best topic sentence for the paragraph.
_____ **He plays a large role in making America's laws, since he approves laws that Congress creates. He also has the important duty of being in charge of the military. As the leader of the nation, the president is in charge of all government workers. It is clear that the role of the president impacts every one of us.**
    Ⓐ In one way or another, the president makes decisions that affect every citizen.
    Ⓑ The president has a hard job.
    Ⓒ The president has the power to veto a bill.
    Ⓓ Until 1951, the president could have been elected to as many terms as he wanted.

6 What is wrong with the paragraph in number 5?
    Ⓐ most sentences start the same
    Ⓑ too many simple words should have been changed using synonyms
    Ⓒ the sentences are all too short and choppy
    Ⓓ none of the above

PREWRITE
Turn this paper over, and draw a line to divide your paper in half. Label the two sides *Pros* and *Cons*. List three advantadges and three disadvantadges related to the job of the president.

QUICKWRITE
If given the chance, would you want to be the president of the United States as an adult? Why or why not?

Writing Warm-up 11

1 Underline the verbs in the sentence below.

It is easy being a child, since you don't have to pay bills, cook meals, or work for a company.

2 Edit the following sentence, and rewrite it on the line below.

i need to take a snak to the movies or ill be starving

_____

3 Which word is **not** a synonym for *change*?

Ⓐ alter   Ⓑ adjust   Ⓒ adapt   Ⓓ continue

4 Revise the sentence below.

Do you like the tree house my dad and I builded?

_____

5 Choose the best topic sentence for the paragraph.

_____ **You get to play as soon as your homework is finished. You are more relaxed, since you are not responsible for other people. You get more sleep than your parents. I like being a kid!**

Ⓐ It's great being a kid!

Ⓑ People change their attitudes as they grow and mature.

Ⓒ Growing up is hard.

Ⓓ There are many benefits of being an adult.

6 What is wrong with the paragraph in number 5?

Ⓐ most sentences start the same

Ⓑ too many simple words should have been changed using synonyms

Ⓒ the sentences are all too short and choppy

Ⓓ none of the above

PREWRITE
Turn this paper over, and draw a line dividing your paper in half. Label the two sides *Pros* and *Cons*. List three advantages and three disadvantages of being a child.

QUICKWRITE
If given the chance, would you stay your current age forever? Why or why not?

Writing Warm-up 12

1 Underline the verbs in the sentence below.
If you want to become a pilot, then you must first earn a license.

2 Edit the following sentence, and rewrite it on the line below.
do you have enouf experience flying planes to earn a license

_____

3 Which word is **not** a synonym for *practice*?
Ⓐ train   Ⓑ repeat   Ⓒ prepare   Ⓓ transport

4 Revise the sentence below.
The need for good pilots is still grown in some private airline companies.

_____

5 Choose the best topic sentence for the paragraph.
_____ **You must pass a basic medical exam. You also must be able to read, speak, and understand English, because it is the international language of aviation. As far as age is concerned, you must be at least 17 years old. Finally, you must complete a minimum of 40 hours of flight time. If you meet these requirements, then you can become a pilot!**
Ⓐ Pilots get to fly anywhere in the world at no cost.
Ⓑ Getting a pilot's license can be fun.
Ⓒ There are many requirements you must meet before earning a pilot's license.
Ⓓ Many companies are looking for good pilots.

6 What is wrong with the paragraph in number 5?
Ⓐ most sentences start the same
Ⓑ too many simple words should have been changed using synonyms
Ⓒ the sentences are all too short and choppy
Ⓓ none of the above

PREWRITE Turn this paper over, and draw a line dividing your paper in half. Label the two sides *Pros* and *Cons*. List three advantages and three disadvantages of being a pilot.

QUICKWRITE If given the chance, would you want to fly an airplane? Why or why not?

Writing Warm-up 13

1 Underline the verbs in the sentence below.
In general, children require more sleep than adults.

2 Edit the following sentence, and rewrite it on the line below.
do you find it dificult to fall asleep at bedtime

_____

3 Which word is **not** a synonym for *tired*?
    Ⓐ energized   Ⓑ sleepy   Ⓒ exhausted   Ⓓ fatigued

4 Revise the sentence below.
Do you think you need more sleep as you growed older?

_____

5 Choose the best topic sentence for the paragraph.
_____ Your alertness goes down and you are often less creative. Your mind doesn't have time to repair itself. Your immune system does not get the boost it needs. Therefore, it's important to get plenty of sleep every night.
    Ⓐ By sleeping more each night, your body has more time
       to repair itself.
    Ⓑ Sleep helps your brain relax.
    Ⓒ Not getting enough sleep can be harmful to your health.
    Ⓓ The optimal amount of sleep is eight hours per night.

6 What is wrong with the paragraph in number 5?
    Ⓐ most sentences start the same
    Ⓑ too many simple words should have been changed using synonyms
    Ⓒ the sentences are all too short and choppy
    Ⓓ none of the above

PREWRITE
Turn this paper over, and draw a line dividing your paper in half. Label the two sides *Pros* and *Cons*. List three advantages and three disadvantages of going to bed early.

QUICKWRITE
If given the chance, would you want to change your bedtime to one hour later than it is right now? Why or why not?

Writing Warm-up 14

1 Underline the verbs in the sentence below.
People who live in different states get a chance to meet many different people.

2 Edit the following sentence, and rewrite it on the line below.
did you know that a drivers lisense allows you to drive in any state

_____

3 Which word is **not** a synonym for *same*?
    Ⓐ similar   Ⓑ duplicate   Ⓒ alike   Ⓓ changing

4 Revise the sentence below.
The home team was hit the ball so hard that the visiting team had no chance of winning.

_____

5 Choose the best topic sentence for the paragraph.
_____ **When you are the new kid, sometimes you don't feel welcome. It can be difficult when the other children have known each other for a long time. Then, just when you have made new friends, it is time to move again.**
    Ⓐ It's hard to make new friends when you move all the time.
    Ⓑ Living in different states helps you make more friends.
    Ⓒ Many people enjoy moving around from state to state.
    Ⓓ As you travel, you get to see new parts of the nation.

6 What is wrong with the paragraph in number 5?
    Ⓐ most sentences start the same
    Ⓑ too many simple words should have been changed using synonyms
    Ⓒ the sentences are all too short and choppy
    Ⓓ none of the above

PREWRITE Turn this paper over, and draw a line dividing your paper in half. Label the two sides *Pros* and *Cons*. List three advantages and three disadvantages of moving from state to state during the year.

QUICKWRITE If given the chance, would you want to move to a new state? Why or why not?

Writing Warm-up 15

1 Underline the verbs in the sentence below.
   The menu included chicken nuggets, pizza, and meatball sandwiches.

2 Edit the following sentence, and rewrite it on the line below.
   would you beleve me if i told you that theyre taking chicken nuggets off the menu

_____

3 Which word is **not** a synonym for *yummy*?
   Ⓐ tasty   Ⓑ delicious   Ⓒ flavorful   Ⓓ gorgeous

4 Revise the sentence below.
   All of the students cheered when they saw the yummy cupcakes on the menu.

_____

5 Choose the best topic sentence for the paragraph.
   _____ **The results were interesting. Chicken nuggets were most popular. Many students liked turkey. Some voted for pizza. Only three people liked sandwiches. They created a new menu.**
   Ⓐ Weaver Elementary just conducted a survey to determine favorite cafeteria food items.
   Ⓑ Most students at Weaver Elementary School eat in the cafeteria.
   Ⓒ The most popular cafeteria food isn't pizza.
   Ⓓ Brownies were more popular than cookies.

6 What is wrong with the paragraph in number 5?
   Ⓐ most sentences start the same
   Ⓑ too many simple words should have been changed using synonyms
   Ⓒ the sentences are all too short and choppy
   Ⓓ none of the above

PREWRITE Turn this paper over, and draw a line dividing your paper in half. Label the two sides *Pros* and *Cons*. List three advantages and three disadvantages of creating a cafeteria menu.

QUICKWRITE If given the chance, would you want to plan a menu for the cafeteria? Why or why not? If you did, what foods would you choose and why?

Daily Writing Warm-ups 3–4 © 2006 Creative Teaching Press

Writing Warm-up 16

1 Underline the verbs in the sentence below.
The purpose of the military is to protect the country.

2 Edit the following sentence, and rewrite it on the line below.
he finaly received the letter saying he was accepted into the united states air forse

_____

3 Which word is **not** a synonym for *big* as in "a *big* job"?
     Ⓐ useless   Ⓑ important   Ⓒ essential   Ⓓ large

4 Revise the sentence below.
Do you think he's growed up enough for such a big responsibility?

_____

5 Choose the best topic sentence for the paragraph.
_____ The army defends the country on land. The navy defends the country from the water. The air force defends the country from the air. These are some of the branches of the military that protect our country.

     Ⓐ There are different branches of the military.
     Ⓑ The military includes many important jobs.
     Ⓒ Being in the military requires hard work, dedication, and bravery.
     Ⓓ Military personnel have many important duties.

6 What is wrong with the paragraph in number 5?
     Ⓐ most sentences start the same
     Ⓑ too many simple words should have been changed using synonyms
     Ⓒ the sentences are all too short and choppy
     Ⓓ none of the above

PREWRITE Turn this paper over, and draw a line dividing your paper in half. Label the two sides *Pros* and *Cons*. List three advantages and three disadvantages of being in the military.

QUICKWRITE If given the chance, would you join a branch of the military? Why or why not?

Writing Warm-up 17

1 Underline the verbs in the sentence below.
Her brother wanted to sail across the ocean to an island.

2 Edit the following sentence, and rewrite it on the line below.
she alway asks her mother for advise before making important decisions

_____

3 Which word is **not** a synonym for *big* as in "a *big* ship"?
    Ⓐ large   Ⓑ important   Ⓒ massive   Ⓓ enormous

4 Revise the sentence below.
The captain buyed rafts and life jackets for the big ship.

_____

5 Choose the best topic sentence for the paragraph.
_____ **Some like the ocean breeze. Others like to compete in races. Some think you get a lot of exercise. Others enjoy exploring. Sailing is an exciting sport.**
    Ⓐ Being on a sailboat allows you to enjoy nature and the ocean.
    Ⓑ Sailing is one of the most adventurous things a person can do.
    Ⓒ Sailing is very expensive but rewarding.
    Ⓓ People sail for many different reasons.

6 What is wrong with the paragraph in number 5?
    Ⓐ most sentences start the same
    Ⓑ too many simple words should have been changed using synonyms
    Ⓒ the sentences are all too short and choppy
    Ⓓ none of the above

PREWRITE Turn this paper over, and draw a line dividing your paper in half. Label the two sides *Pros* and *Cons*. List three advantages and three disadvantages of sailing a boat or yacht.

QUICKWRITE If given the chance, would you take a year off from school to sail around the world? Why or why not?

Name_____   Date _____

Writing Warm-up 18

1 Underline the verbs in the sentence below.
His principal called him into the office after he said a bad word at school.

2 Edit the following sentence, and rewrite it on the line below.
he usualy didnt say bad words, but when he did, was disciplined

_____

3 Which word is **not** a synonym for *fair* as in "a *fair* principal"?
    Ⓐ just   Ⓑ impartial   Ⓒ biased   Ⓓ virtuous

4 Revise the sentence below.
The boy hitted the girl after she taked the ball from him.

_____

5 Choose the best topic sentence for the paragraph.
_____ **The principal must discipline children. She also leads meetings. In addition, she is in charge of the teachers and plans the school budget. Principals work hard for their schools.**
    Ⓐ A school principal should be friendly and fair.
    Ⓑ A school principal has many important duties.
    Ⓒ What is your principal like?
    Ⓓ Have you ever been to the principal's office?

6 What is wrong with the paragraph in number 5?
    Ⓐ most sentences start the same
    Ⓑ too many simple words should have been changed
        using synonyms
    Ⓒ the sentences are all too short and choppy
    Ⓓ none of the above

PREWRITE
Turn this paper over, and draw a line dividing your paper in half. Label the two sides *Pros* and *Cons*. List three advantages and three disadvantages of being a school principal.

QUICKWRITE
If given the chance, would you want to be the principal of your school? Why or why not?

QUIZ 2

1 Underline any verbs in the sentence below.
Amy had to make her bed, wash the dishes, and sweep the porch.

2 Edit the following sentence, and rewrite it on the line below.
did she had a dificult time deciding which vacuum to buy at the store

_____

3 Which word is **not** a synonym for _big_ as in "a _big_ responsibility"?
Ⓐ important
Ⓑ meaningless
Ⓒ essential
Ⓓ needed

4 Revise the sentence below.
She got a good award at home, because she hitted the ball the farthest in the game.

_____

_____

5 Write a topic sentence for the paragraph.

_____

First, she decided to start off with changing the foods she ate. She stopped eating chips and cookies every day because they had too many wasted calories. Next, she joined a gym to exercise and improve her heart rate. Finally, Lisa began to notice her weight going down. Her diet was working!

6 What is wrong with the paragraph in number 5?
Ⓐ most sentences start the same
Ⓑ too many simple words should have been changed using synonyms
Ⓒ the sentences are all too short and choppy
Ⓓ none of the above

Show what you know!

SCORE

Daily Writing Warm-ups 3–4 © 2006 Creative Teaching Press

Name_____   Date _____

Writing Warm-up 19

1 Underline any nouns and circle any verbs in the sentence below.
She loved to eat cookies and drink soda.

2 Edit the following sentence, and rewrite it on the line below.
its not a good idea to eat cookies candy pretzels and chocolate before dinner

_____

3 Which word is **not** a synonym for *eat*?
 Ⓐ eliminate Ⓑ devour   © munch   Ⓓ gobble

4 Revise the sentence below.
They wanted to eat the yummy cookies, but they knowed their baby brother would tell.

_____

5 Choose the best concluding sentence for the paragraph.
Linda was crazy about dessert. There wasn't a sweet treat Linda wouldn't eat. She would eat only dessert if she could. Peanut butter cookies were her favorite. Raspberry hot chocolate was also a favorite treat. Whenever she went to a restaurant, she chose her dessert first. _____

 Ⓐ Linda loved dessert more than anything.
 Ⓑ She also enjoyed eating chocolate chip cookies.
 © Her favorite dessert was pie.
 Ⓓ What would she order?

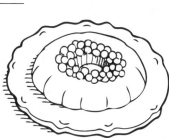

6 What is wrong with the paragraph in number 5?
 Ⓐ it sounds robotic (boring and repetitive)
 Ⓑ the vocabulary is too simple; some words should be revised
 © it jumps around too much, so the paragraph doesn't flow well
 Ⓓ none of the above

PREWRITE
Turn this paper over, and draw three boxes. Label each box with a favorite dessert. List three reasons why you like each dessert.

QUICKWRITE
If you could eat a sweet treat every day for dessert, what would it be? Why?

Name_____ Date _____

Writing Warm-up 20

1 Underline any nouns and circle any verbs in the sentence below.
She slurped her spaghetti and burped at the dinner table!

2 Edit the following sentence, and rewrite it on the line below.
she couldnt beleive that the girl just burped for the forth time

_____

3 Which word is **not** a synonym for *gross*?
Ⓐ amazing   Ⓑ disgusting   Ⓒ unpleasant   Ⓓ yucky

4 Revise the sentence below.
Those children sure needs lessons on good manners.

_____

5 Choose the best concluding sentence for the paragraph.
People will often judge you based on your manners. If you burp in public, then people will find you rude. If you yell at a waiter, then people will think you are disrespectful. If you chew with your mouth open, then people won't want to eat with you. _____
Ⓐ If you want to make a good impression, remember to use good manners.
Ⓑ Manners matter.
Ⓒ Poor manners are disgusting.
Ⓓ Use good manners.

6 What is wrong with the paragraph in number 5?
Ⓐ it sounds robotic (boring and repetitive)
Ⓑ the vocabulary is too simple; some words should be revised
Ⓒ it jumps around too much, so it doesn't flow well
Ⓓ none of the above

Excuse me

PREWRITE Turn this paper over, and draw four boxes. Label each box with an example of a good manner you have observed.

QUICKWRITE Why do you think it is important to use good manners? Describe a time when you used good manners.

Daily Writing Warm-ups 3–4 © 2006 Creative Teaching Press

Writing Warm-up 21

1 Underline any nouns and circle any verbs in the sentence below.
Many people dip their sandwich cookies in milk until they get soggy.

2 Edit the following sentence, and rewrite it on the line below.
he easily twisted the top off the cookie and then licked the frosting

_____

3 Which word is **not** a synonym for _make_?
    Ⓐ prepare   Ⓑ aware   Ⓒ create   Ⓓ form

4 Revise the sentence below.
They taked the cookies out of the package and eated them all before dinner.

_____

5 Choose the best concluding sentence for the paragraph.
How do you eat cookies? Do you dip them in milk? Do you twist off the tops? Do you chew around the outside first? Do you just bite into them? _____

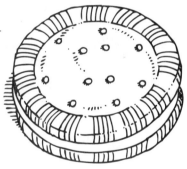

    Ⓐ There are many different kinds of cookies.
    Ⓑ Cookies are delicious treats!
    Ⓒ Cookies are popular treats.
    Ⓓ Cookies can be eaten many interesting ways.

6 What is wrong with the paragraph in number 5?
    Ⓐ it sounds robotic (boring and repetitive)
    Ⓑ the vocabulary is too simple; some words should be revised
    Ⓒ it jumps around too much, so it doesn't flow well
    Ⓓ none of the above

PREWRITE
Turn this paper over, and draw three boxes. Label each box with an example of how to eat a sandwich cookie. Put a star next to the one you like best.

QUICKWRITE
What is the best way to eat a sandwich cookie? Explain in detail, step by step, as if someone were going to do it with you.

Writing Warm-up 22

1 Underline any nouns and circle any verbs in the sentence below.
   She always eats french fries with her hamburgers.

2 Edit the following sentence, and rewrite it on the line below.
   do you no that she usualy eats there at least once a week

_____

3 Which word is **not** a synonym for *open* as in "*open* a restaurant"?
   Ⓐ disrupt   Ⓑ launch   Ⓒ start   Ⓓ begin

4 Revise the sentence below.
   The neighbors told the city that they needed some good fast-food restaurants in their town.

_____

5 Choose the best concluding sentence for the paragraph.
   It takes a lot of hard work to open a fast-food restaurant. First, a person has to choose the type of restaurant he or she wants. A lot of money is needed to pay for the land and name. The person needs to take hard classes on budgeting and managing people. Workers must be hired. _____
   Ⓐ After these things are completed, a store can be opened.
   Ⓑ Many steps are involved in opening a fast-food restaurant.
   Ⓒ Wow! So much work!
   Ⓓ Could you do that?

6 What is wrong with the paragraph in number 5?
   Ⓐ it sounds robotic (boring and repetitive)
   Ⓑ the vocabulary is too simple; some words should be revised
   Ⓒ it jumps around too much, so it doesn't flow well
   Ⓓ none of the above

PREWRITE
Turn this paper over, and draw three boxes. Label each box with the name of a favorite fast-food restaurant. List three reasons why you like each one.

QUICKWRITE
Which fast-food restaurant would you love to have near your home? Why?

Daily Writing Warm-ups 3–4 © 2006 Creative Teaching Press

Writing Warm-up 23

1 Underline any nouns and circle any verbs in the sentence below.
In the summer, many people eat ice-cream sundaes.

2 Edit the following sentence, and rewrite it on the line below.
would you eat ice cream even tho you were allergic to dairy products

_____

3 Which word is **not** a synonym for *cold* as in "*cold* ice cream"?
Ⓐ mean   Ⓑ chilly   Ⓒ frozen   Ⓓ frosty

4 Revise the sentence below.
The kids thinked of good toppings for their cold sundaes.

_____

5 Choose the best concluding sentence for the paragraph.
Ice cream is made from a few key ingredients. Milk is the main product. Ice is also needed. Sugar and vanilla are needed too. _____
Ⓐ It really is that simple to make ice cream.
Ⓑ With these few ingredients, you can make ice cream.
Ⓒ That is all you need to make ice cream, especially if you like vanilla.
Ⓓ I love ice cream!

6 What is wrong with the paragraph in number 5?
Ⓐ it sounds robotic (boring and repetitive)
Ⓑ the vocabulary is too simple; some words should be revised
Ⓒ it jumps around too much, so it doesn't flow well
Ⓓ none of the above

PREWRITE Turn this paper over, and draw four boxes. Label each with the name of a favorite ice-cream sundae topping.

QUICKWRITE You're about to become famous! A local ice-cream store wants to name a sundae after you. What should it be called? What ingredients should be included?

Name_____   Date _____

Writing Warm-up 24

1 Underline any nouns and circle any verbs in the sentence below.
Jalapenos are hot peppers often used in spicy dishes.

2 Edit the following sentence, and rewrite it on the line below.
is it true that the chef is triing to devellop a new recipe using jalapeno peppers

_____

3 Which word is **not** an antonym for *hot* as in *"hot* salsa"?
    Ⓐ mild   Ⓑ spicy   Ⓒ bland   Ⓓ weak

4 Revise the sentence below.
Chef Norton was thought she had a new twist for making good breadsticks.

_____

5 Choose the best concluding sentence for the paragraph.
Jalapeno peppers are famous in Texas. The jalapeno is one of the official state peppers. Jalapeno pepper jelly originated in Lake Jackson, Texas. In fact, if you go there, you'll taste many unique food items made with jalapenos. You should visit if you like jalapenos. _____
    Ⓐ Texans love their jalapenos!
    Ⓑ Bring some water with you, because your mouth will be burning.
    Ⓒ Jalapeno pepper jelly was created in 1978.
    Ⓓ Texas is the largest state on the mainland and famous for jalapenos.

6 What is wrong with the paragraph in number 5?
    Ⓐ it sounds robotic (boring and repetitive)
    Ⓑ the vocabulary is too simple; some words should
         be revised
    Ⓒ it jumps around too much, so it doesn't flow well
    Ⓓ none of the above

PREWRITE
Turn this paper over, and sketch a jalapeno pizza. All around the outside crust, list reasons why you would or would not eat a slice of jalapeno pizza.

QUICKWRITE
Would you eat jalapeno pizza? Why or why not? Give at least three reasons explaining your answer.

Daily Writing Warm-ups 3–4 © 2006 Creative Teaching Press

Writing Warm-up 25

1 Underline any nouns and circle any verbs in the sentence below.
Carina loves to eat Italian food, but her brother likes Mexican food the best.

2 Edit the following sentence, and rewrite it on the line below.
getting the right quanttity of noodles onions and zucchini in the stir-fry mix is important

_____

3 Which word is **not** an antonym for *different*?
    Ⓐ similar   Ⓑ various   Ⓒ alike   Ⓓ comparable

4 Revise the sentence below.
She liked many different foods as long as they tasted good.

_____

5 Choose the best concluding sentence for the paragraph.
Mexican food is a popular dinner choice for children. Most children like tacos. Burritos are also very popular, especially when filled with ground beef. Some children think enchiladas are good, too. _____
    Ⓐ What they don't like as much is refried beans.
    Ⓑ Children often choose Mexican food when given a choice for dinner.
    Ⓒ Therefore, tacos, burritos, and enchiladas are popular with kids.
    Ⓓ Mexican food has been growing in popularity.

6 What is wrong with the paragraph in number 5?
    Ⓐ it sounds robotic (boring and repetitive)
    Ⓑ the vocabulary is too simple; some words
        should be revised
    Ⓒ it jumps around too much, so it doesn't flow well
    Ⓓ none of the above

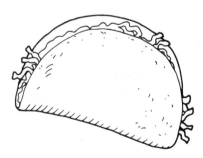

PREWRITE Turn this paper over, and draw four boxes. In each box label a favorite dinner food.

QUICKWRITE What is your favorite type of food? Do you prefer Italian, Vietnamese, Mexican, or some other type of food? What specific foods do you like? Why?

Name_____   Date _____

Writing Warm-up 26

1 Underline any nouns and circle any verbs in the sentence below.
On the cruise, she ordered dessert before dinner so she would not be too full to enjoy it.

2 Edit the following sentence, and rewrite it on the line below.
when eating a meal should you begin with the salad the main course or the dessert

_____

3 Which word is **not** an antonym for *asked*?
Ⓐ answered   Ⓑ requested   Ⓒ replied   Ⓓ responded

4 Revise the sentence below.
She asked the waiter, "Would you please showed me the dessert tray?"

_____

5 Choose the best concluding sentence for the paragraph.
Believe it or not, some desserts are healthy foods. A fresh fruit pie is good for you as long as it isn't loaded with sugar. Peanut butter and banana is healthy and nutritious. That reminds me of my favorite dessert. Do you like butterscotch apples? Fresh fruit is a delicious and healthy dessert choice. _____
Ⓐ Although dessert is often considered unhealthy, some choices are good for you.
Ⓑ My favorite dessert is hot apple pie.
Ⓒ Maybe you prefer to eat a bowl of fresh berries.
Ⓓ There are not any desserts that are healthy foods.

6 What is wrong with the paragraph in number 5?
Ⓐ it sounds robotic (boring and repetitive)
Ⓑ the vocabulary is too simple; some words should be revised
Ⓒ it jumps around too much, so it doesn't flow well
Ⓓ none of the above

PREWRITE
Turn this paper over, and draw four boxes. In each box, list a favorite dessert item that could be considered healthy.

QUICKWRITE
If you were given the chance, would you eat dessert before dinner? In which cases would you say "yes"? When would you say "no"?

38

Daily Writing Warm-ups 3–4 © 2006 Creative Teaching Press

Writing Warm-up 27

1 Underline any nouns and circle any verbs in the sentence below.
I think this salad tastes great!

2 Edit the following sentence, and rewrite it on the line below.
if your thru with your plates, then ill go wash the dishes put them away and bring out dessert

_____

3 Which word is **not** an antonym for *loved*?
Ⓐ despised   Ⓑ detested   Ⓒ loathed   Ⓓ adored

4 Revise the sentence below.
He told the waiter he would like to order soup.

_____

5 Choose the best concluding sentence for the paragraph.
I remember the special birthday dinner my mom prepared. She had asked me what I wanted to eat. Since it was my birthday, I asked for her famous barbecue chicken dinner with mashed potatoes. She made the best barbecue sauce. I even had my favorite dessert, strawberry shortcake. _____
Ⓐ My mom served canned cranberry sauce.
Ⓑ The dessert was the best!
Ⓒ Everyone enjoyed my birthday dinner.
Ⓓ That birthday dinner was the best!

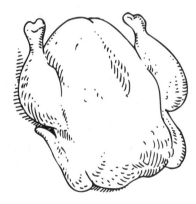

6 What is wrong with the paragraph in number 5?
Ⓐ it sounds robotic (boring and repetitive)
Ⓑ the vocabulary is too simple; some words should be revised
Ⓒ it jumps around too much, so it doesn't flow well
Ⓓ none of the above

PREWRITE Turn this paper over, and draw four boxes. Label the boxes *appetizer, soup/salad, main dish,* and *dessert*. In each box, list your favorite foods.

QUICKWRITE What is the best dinner you've ever had? Include foods you listed in your boxes. Why did you enjoy the dinner so much?

QUIZ 3

1 Underline any verbs and circle any nouns in the sentence below.
Before the earthquake, Lynn's rabbit thumped and her dog barked loudly.

2 Edit the following sentence, and rewrite it on the line below.
would you rather picnic in the park swim in a pool or collect shells at the beach

_____

3 Which word is **not** an antonym for *asked?*
Ⓐ replied
Ⓑ requested
Ⓒ responded
Ⓓ answered

4 Revise the sentence below.
Did you hear that she told the teacher that her friends were talked behind her back?

_____

_____

5 Write a concluding sentence for the paragraph.
Household tasks are an important part of growing up. By doing a chore around the house, you demonstrate that you are responsible. You also show that you care about the upkeep of the house. You prove that you respect your family by doing chores.

_____

6 What is wrong with the paragraph in number 5?
Ⓐ it sounds robotic (boring and repetitive)
Ⓑ the vocabulary is too simple; some words should be revised
Ⓒ it jumps around too much, so it doesn't flow well
Ⓓ none of the above

Give it your all!

SCORE

Daily Writing Warm-ups 3–4 © 2006 Creative Teaching Press

Writing Warm-up 28

1 Underline any pronouns in the sentence below.
Where in the world did she ever find such bright green pants?

2 Edit the following sentence, and rewrite it on the line below.
wood you mind helping me by took this shirt to the cleaners after work

_____

3 Which word is **not** a synonym for _odd_?
Ⓐ common   Ⓑ weird   Ⓒ unusual   Ⓓ strange

4 Revise the sentence below.
Her odd-looking pair of pants got the attention of all the kids in hers class.

_____

5 Choose the best concluding sentence for the paragraph.
If you wear blue jeans, then you should thank Levi Strauss. He invented them in 1848 during the Gold Rush. He was a cloth seller who journeyed west from New York with some of his cloth. When it ran out, he made pants out of canvas. Later, he switched from canvas to jeans. He created the first pair of blue jeans. _____
Ⓐ Today, if you wear blue jeans, remember to think of Levi Strauss.
Ⓑ Levi Strauss created a useful invention.
Ⓒ I love Levi Strauss.
Ⓓ Levi Strauss created the blue jeans for miners and cowboys, but now we all wear them.

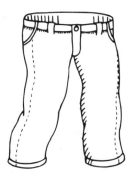

6 What is wrong with the paragraph in number 5?
Ⓐ it sounds robotic (boring and repetitive)
Ⓑ the vocabulary is too simple; some words should be revised
Ⓒ it jumps around too much, so it doesn't flow well
Ⓓ none of the above

PREWRITE
Turn this paper over, and sketch what you normally wear to school.

QUICKWRITE
Never say never! What design or color of pants would you never wear? Why? What might make you change your mind?

Writing Warm-up 29

1 Underline any pronouns in the sentence below.
They must take classes to earn their Firefighter Academy certificates.

2 Edit the following sentence, and rewrite it on the line below.
does the postal worker standing over their look familliar

_____

3 Which word or phrase is **not** a synonym for *rarely*?
    Ⓐ seldom   Ⓑ often   © infrequently   Ⓓ hardly ever

4 Revise the sentence below.
She rarely had any free time, since her hard job kept her very busy all day.

_____

5 Choose the best concluding sentence for the paragraph.
There are many things to think about before picking a job. It is smart to think about what you are good at doing. What do you want to be when you grow up? How much money will you get paid? You should also think about the positive and negative points of the job. Will you have to work long and hard days? Will the job make you happy?

_____
    Ⓐ Working hard earns you money.
    Ⓑ Will you keep that job forever?
    © In any job, you'll find benefits and drawbacks.
    Ⓓ Be smart.

6 What is wrong with the paragraph in number 5?
    Ⓐ it sounds robotic (boring and repetitive)
    Ⓑ the vocabulary is too simple; some words should be revised
    © it jumps around too much, so it doesn't flow well
    Ⓓ none of the above

PREWRITE
Turn this paper over, and draw four boxes. In each box, write the name of a job that you think would be fun to have. List three reasons why under each job.

QUICKWRITE
Never say never! When you grow up, what job do you think would be difficult to get but that you would love to do? Why?

Daily Writing Warm-ups 3–4 © 2006 Creative Teaching Press

Writing Warm-up 30

1 Underline any pronouns in the sentence below.
Television is the worst invention of all time, since it makes people lazy.

2 Edit the following sentence, and rewrite it on the line below.
how offin do you watch television instead of play outside

_____

3 Which word is **not** a synonym for *wasted* as in *"wasted* time"?
ⓐ useless   ⓑ meaningful   ⓒ futile   ⓓ worthless

4 Revise the sentence below.
He taked his time doing his homework so his dad wouldn't says he didn't use hisin time well.

_____

5 Choose the best concluding sentence for the paragraph.
Most households have at least one television. Many TV sets even have built-in DVD players. Television viewing has increased every decade. Televisions are now sometimes found in kitchens. A survey found that over 95% of American homes have at least one TV. _____
ⓐ Therefore, television viewing is more popular today than ever before.
ⓑ The content and language of many shows has also changed over time.
ⓒ Therefore, most homes have at least one television.
ⓓ That leaves about 5% of the population without a television.

6 What is wrong with the paragraph in number 5?
ⓐ it sounds robotic (boring and repetitive)
ⓑ the vocabulary is too simple; some words should be revised
ⓒ it jumps around too much, so it doesn't flow well
ⓓ none of the above

PREWRITE Turn this paper over, and draw a line down the middle. On the left, write your favorite TV show. On the right, name a show you would never watch. List three reasons why you like or dislike each show.

QUICKWRITE Never say never! Which TV show do you think you would never want to watch? Why? What might make you change your mind?

Writing Warm-up 31

1 Underline any pronouns in the sentence below.
Her bad habit is that she is constantly biting her nails.

2 Edit the following sentence, and rewrite it on the line below.
people offin devellop bad habits without even realizeing it

_____

3 Which word is **not** a synonym for *dumb* as in *"dumb* idea"?
    Ⓐ clever   Ⓑ foolish   Ⓒ ridiculous   Ⓓ absurd

4 Revise the sentence below.
What a dumb idea to let the clothes pile up for a month before washed thems.

_____

5 Choose the best concluding sentence for the paragraph.
Most people admit that they have at least one bad habit. Some people tap their nails while people are talking. Some people say bad words. Some people are constantly licking their lips. Some people snap their gum. Do you have any of these bad habits?

    Ⓐ If not, you can probably admit to at least one other bad habit.
    Ⓑ Many people have bad habits.
    Ⓒ What are your bad habits?
    Ⓓ Bad habits are hard to break.

6 What is wrong with the paragraph in number 5?
    Ⓐ it sounds robotic (boring and repetitive)
    Ⓑ the vocabulary is too simple; some words should be revised
    Ⓒ it jumps around too much, so it doesn't flow well
    Ⓓ none of the above

PREWRITE Turn this paper over, and make a list of six bad habits. Cross out any that you would never develop. Circle the ones that you admit to having.

QUICKWRITE Never say never! Which bad habit do you think you'll never develop? Why? Would there be anything that might cause you to develop that habit?

Daily Writing Warm-ups 3–4 © 2006 Creative Teaching Press

Writing Warm-up 32

1 Underline any pronouns in the sentence below.
Do you know what his favorite sport might be?

2 Edit the following sentence, and rewrite it on the line below.
she was begining to thinked that she might want to try out for soccer after all

_____

3 Which word is **not** a synonym for _fun_ as in "a _fun_ sport"?
Ⓐ exciting   Ⓑ entertaining   Ⓒ engaging   Ⓓ beautiful

4 Revise the sentence below.
She thought basketball was a fun sport, but she wasn't sure she would be good at it.

_____

5 Choose the best concluding sentence for the paragraph.
The Olympic Games are an example of international sporting competitions. The Olympics have an official flag, motto, oath, and flame. The top three finishers in each event earn a gold, silver, or bronze medal. The purpose of the Olympics is to allow the best athletes from around the world to compete against one another. _____
Ⓐ The Olympics provide unique, exciting opportunities for the world's top athletes.
Ⓑ The Olympics originated in Greece, but now they are international.
Ⓒ The international competition occurs every four years.
Ⓓ Therefore, the Olympics have a long and important history.

6 What is wrong with the paragraph in number 5?
Ⓐ it sounds robotic (boring and repetitive)
Ⓑ the vocabulary is too simple; some words should be revised
Ⓒ it jumps around too much, so it doesn't flow well
Ⓓ none of the above

PREWRITE Turn this paper over, and list ten sports. Circle the sports you would be willing to try (including ones you have tried). Cross out the sports you would never try.

QUICKWRITE Never say never! Which sport do you think you'll never try? Why? Is there anything that might make you change your mind?

Writing Warm-up 33

1 Underline any pronouns in the sentence below.
Malts are ice-cream shakes with malted milk added to them.

2 Edit the following sentence, and rewrite it on the line below.
he told her that his favorit beverages are lemonade milk and juice

_____

3 Which word is **not** a synonym for *bad* as in *"bad* for you"?
ⓐ dangerous   ⓑ unhealthy   ⓒ beneficial   ⓓ hazardous

4 Revise the sentence below.
Do you agree with mine think that he shouldn't drink soda until he's a teenager?

_____

5 Choose the best concluding sentence for the paragraph.
**The survey had interesting results. The most popular
beverage chosen by children was juice. The most popular
drink chosen by teenagers was soda. The most popular
beverage among adults was coffee. The researchers realized
that as people get older, they make more unhealthful choices.**

_____
ⓐ That was a surprising discovery of the survey.
ⓑ What do you like to drink?
ⓒ The results of the survey were interesting.
ⓓ Beverage companies will use the information for marketing purposes.

6 What is wrong with the paragraph in number 5?
ⓐ it sounds robotic (boring and repetitive)
ⓑ the vocabulary is too simple; some words should be revised
ⓒ it jumps around too much, so it doesn't flow well
ⓓ none of the above

PREWRITE
Turn this paper over, and
list ten beverages. Circle
the drinks you enjoy.
Cross out the beverages
you would never try.

QUICKWRITE
Never say never! Which
drink do you think you'll
never try? Why? What
might make you change
your mind?

Daily Writing Warm-ups 3–4 © 2006 Creative Teaching Press

Writing Warm-up 34

1 Underline any pronouns in the sentence below.
In some countries, people live in huts or tents they build themselves.

2 Edit the following sentence, and rewrite it on the line below.
wood you chose to live on a island in the dessert or on a ranch

_____

3 Which word is **not** a synonym for *nice* as in "a *nice* house"?
    Ⓐ friendly   Ⓑ comfortable   © cozy   Ⓓ satisfying

4 Revise the sentence below.
Do you think a tent is a nice place to live, or do you think a tent is a bad home?

_____

5 Choose the best concluding sentence for the paragraph.
There are many kinds of homes. In Australia, some people live in apartments called "flats." Tents are used for homes in Afghanistan. Some people in Europe live in large homes called estates. _____
    Ⓐ In countries around the world, some people don't even have a home at all.
    Ⓑ In the United States, there are many different kinds of homes.
    © Around the world, people live in different kinds of homes.
    Ⓓ Despite the differences, everyone needs shelter.

6 What is wrong with the paragraph in number 5?
    Ⓐ it sounds robotic (boring and repetitive)
    Ⓑ the vocabulary is too simple; some words should be revised
    © it jumps around too much, so it doesn't flow well
    Ⓓ none of the above

PREWRITE Turn this paper over, and draw a line down the middle. On the left, list three places where you would love to live some day. On the right, list three places where you would never want to live.

QUICKWRITE Never say never! In which location do you think you'll never live? Why? What might make you change your mind?

Writing Warm-up 35

1 Underline any pronouns in the sentence below.
   While on vacation in Australia, she met a friend with a pet kangaroo.

2 Edit the following sentence, and rewrite it on the line below.
   she thinks shell probly get a pet ferret when she groweds up

_____

3 Which word is **not** a synonym for *cool* as in "a *cool* pet"?
   Ⓐ dull   Ⓑ wonderful   Ⓒ fabulous   Ⓓ marvelous

4 Revise the sentence below.
   Don't you think that a rabbit maked a cool pet for showing a child how to be kind?

_____

5 Choose the best concluding sentence for the paragraph.
   If you ask me, I think that dogs make the best pets. Let me explain. Cats make my allergies flare up. Rats are too small to cuddle. Lizards don't come when I call them. Fish can't be held. Snakes scare my dad. _____
   Ⓐ Rabbits shed too much.
   Ⓑ Therefore, dogs are better than cats.
   Ⓒ So, of all the animals, dogs would make the best pet for me.
   Ⓓ Therefore, dogs make the best pets.

6 What is wrong with the paragraph in number 5?
   Ⓐ it sounds robotic (boring and repetitive)
   Ⓑ the vocabulary is too simple; some words should be revised
   Ⓒ it jumps around too much, so it doesn't flow well
   Ⓓ none of the above

PREWRITE
Turn this paper over, and draw a line down the middle. On the left, list three pets you'd love to have. On the right, list three pets you would never want to have.

QUICKWRITE
Never say never! Which pet would you never want? Why? What might make you change your mind?

Daily Writing Warm-ups 3–4 © 2006 Creative Teaching Press

Writing Warm-up 36

1 Underline any pronouns in the sentence below.
She didn't follow the rules, so her parents had to ground her.

2 Edit the following sentence, and rewrite it on the line below.
you wood be lonly if you losted your friends because you didnt play nicely

_____

3 Which word is **not** a synonym for *bad* as in "a *bad* choice"?
Ⓐ foolish   Ⓑ stinky   Ⓒ unwise   Ⓓ ridiculous

4 Revise the sentence below.
He knowed he made a bad choice when he sayed that his dog ate his homework.

_____

5 Choose the best concluding sentence for the paragraph.
Parents make rules to keep their children safe and to teach life lessons. One important rule is to never talk to strangers. Another rule that keeps children safe is for them to be home at a certain time. Even having a bedtime is a rule that keeps a child's body safe and healthy. _____

Ⓐ Following rules is an important part of growing up.
Ⓑ Rules are made to be broken.
Ⓒ Rules are different in every home.
Ⓓ You should always follow the rules.

6 What is wrong with the paragraph in number 5?
Ⓐ it sounds robotic (boring and repetitive)
Ⓑ the vocabulary is too simple; some words should be revised
Ⓒ it jumps around too much, so it doesn't flow well
Ⓓ none of the above

PREWRITE
Turn this paper over, and write five important rules for staying safe and healthy. Circle the rules you feel are most important.

QUICKWRITE
Never say never! Which rule would you never break? Why? What might make you change your mind?

QUIZ 4

1 Underline any pronouns in the sentence below.
Did you hear her say that she doesn't want to go to the carnival with us?

2 Edit the following sentence, and rewrite it on the line below.
she was shocked when she heard that the amownt of cookies she made was probly not enouf for the hole class

_____

_____

3 Which word is **not** a synonym for *cool* as in "a *cool* jacket"?
Ⓐ tidy
Ⓑ excellent
Ⓒ amazing
Ⓓ interesting

4 Revise the sentence below.
She told the teacher that her slide down the slide backwards.

_____

5 Write a concluding sentence for the paragraph.
Lotion is made up of many different ingredients. Most lotions contain shea butter, which makes your skin smooth. Most also include some type of oil. Most lotions also have water, glycerin, and a fragrance as ingredients.

_____

6 What is wrong with the paragraph in number 5?
Ⓐ it sounds robotic (boring and repetitive)
Ⓑ the vocabulary is too simple; some words should be revised
Ⓒ it jumps around too much, so it doesn't flow well
Ⓓ none of the above

You can do it!

SCORE

Daily Writing Warm-ups 3–4 © 2006 Creative Teaching Press

Writing Warm-up 37

1 Underline any nouns and circle any pronouns in the sentence below.
He couldn't put the book down, because he was finally at the best part.

2 Edit the following sentence, and rewrite it on the line below.
the book lovers club required each member to record the numbr of pages read nightly

_____

3 Which word or phrase is **not** a synonym for *sick of* as in *"sick of* doing that"?
Ⓐ worn out   Ⓑ excited   Ⓒ tired   Ⓓ ill from

4 Revise the sentence below.
He forgetted to return his library book on time, so he was charged a little fine of 25 cents.

_____

5 Which sentence is out of order?
¹Lilly had practiced all night. ²Her oral presentation was even better than she had expected. ³Everyone clapped when she was finished. ⁴It was time to do the oral presentations.
Ⓐ 1   Ⓑ 2   Ⓒ 3   Ⓓ 4

6 "Books inform, entertain, and encourage creative thinking."
Which detail below would **not** support this topic sentence?
Ⓐ Books help answer questions on various topics.
Ⓑ Many people are inspired to invent new things or ideas after reading a terrific book.
Ⓒ Every child should read books from all genres.
Ⓓ When you want to laugh, read a book.

PREWRITE Turn this paper over, and draw five boxes. In each box, list the title of a book you enjoyed. Under each title, list two reasons why you liked the book.

QUICKWRITE Give me five! What are the five best books you have ever read? Explain why.

Name_____ Date _____

Writing Warm-up 38

1 Underline any nouns and circle any pronouns in the sentence below.
Every school has its own plan for improving in the next few years.

2 Edit the following sentence, and rewrite it on the line below.
my calander shows that this weekend is the founders day celebration at lee school

_____

_____

3 Which word or phrase is **not** a synonym for *almost* as in "*almost* done"?
    Ⓐ just about   Ⓑ especially   Ⓒ nearly   Ⓓ practically

4 Revise the sentence below.
You can't going to the school play because yous homework isn't done.

_____

5 Which sentence is out of order?
¹**Jill's report included two creative ideas.** ²**Those two ideas would make the biggest difference in improving the school.** ³**First, the students could create a school-wide behavior plan.** ⁴**Second, there could be a monthly award ceremony for all good school citizens.**
    Ⓐ 1   Ⓑ 2   Ⓒ 3   Ⓓ 4

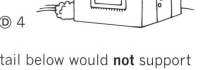

6 "Every school can improve in some way or another." Which detail below would **not** support this topic sentence?
    Ⓐ Some schools need to create better emergency safety procedures.
    Ⓑ Some schools can offer better rewards for good behavior.
    Ⓒ Some schools can recognize individual teachers for their achievements.
    Ⓓ Some schools are already so strong that they don't need to be improved.

PREWRITE Turn this paper over, and draw five boxes. In each box, list one area in which your school could improve. Then list one way your school could reach each goal.

QUICKWRITE Give me five! What are the five ideas for improving your school? Explain each one clearly.

Daily Writing Warm-ups 3–4 © 2006 Creative Teaching Press

Writing Warm-up 39

My Goals:

1 Underline any nouns and circle any pronouns in the sentence below.
He met his goal of making ten baskets in the game.

2 Edit the following sentence, and rewrite it on the line below.
do you have the information abowt the parent conferences

_____

_____

3 Which word or phrase is **not** a synonym for _find_ as in "_find_ the book"?
    Ⓐ discover   Ⓑ locate   Ⓒ lose   Ⓓ come across

4 Revise the sentence below.
I forgotted to write down mine goals for the week, but I remember most of thems.

_____

5 Which sentence is out of order?
[1]He made a set of goals to accomplish over the weekend. [2]He also wanted to mow the lawn, but it rained. [3]The weather, obviously, kept him from meeting his goals! [4]He hoped to plant new roses in the front yard.
    Ⓐ 1   Ⓑ 2   Ⓒ 3   Ⓓ 4

6 "Goals help you stay focused and use your time more efficiently." Which detail below would **not** support this topic sentence?
    Ⓐ If you don't meet your goals, then you should have some consequences.
    Ⓑ By setting a goal, you know what to put higher on a "to do" list.
    Ⓒ Creating goals helps you manage different ideas.
    Ⓓ Goal-setting helps you organize a list of things you want to do.

PREWRITE Turn this paper over, and draw five boxes. In each box, list one goal you hope to accomplish in the next five years.

QUICKWRITE Give me five! What are five goals you'd like to accomplish in the next five years? Why did you choose those goals? How do you plan to reach those goals?

Writing Warm-up 40

1 Underline any nouns and circle any pronouns in the sentence below.
School uniforms are fantastic, since they make getting dressed in the morning so easy.

2 Edit the following sentence, and rewrite it on the line below.
why does evreybody wear those untucked shirts giant belts and baggy jeans

_____

3 Which word is **not** a synonym for *silly* as in "looks *silly*"?
    Ⓐ funny   Ⓑ dangerous   Ⓒ strange   Ⓓ ridiculous

4 Revise the sentence below.
He looked so silly wearing black pants that were ten sizes too big!

_____

5 Which sentence is out of order?
¹It was full of clothes she'd never wear again. ²Gwen left the store with two bags of clothes. ³Her plan was to reorganize her closet to make room for the new clothes. ⁴However, there simply wasn't enough room in the closet.

    Ⓐ 1   Ⓑ 2   Ⓒ 3   Ⓓ 4

6 "School clothing policies are designed with safety in mind." Which detail below would **not** support this topic sentence?
    Ⓐ Children are often allowed to wear whatever they want, since they are encouraged to be creative and independent.
    Ⓑ Some pants are not allowed because they could hide dangerous objects.
    Ⓒ Hats are sometimes banned because they can make it difficult to see clearly.
    Ⓓ Flip flops are not allowed because a student could easily fall or stub a toe.

PREWRITE
Turn this paper over, and draw five boxes. In each box, list one item of clothing that you think would be good for a school uniform.

QUICKWRITE
Give me five! What are five items of clothing you would like to be able to wear for a school uniform? What is your reasoning for each choice?

Daily Writing Warm-ups 3–4 © 2006 Creative Teaching Press

Writing Warm-up 41

1 Underline any nouns and circle any pronouns in the sentence below.
In my opinion, the computer is the greatest invention of all time.

2 Edit the following sentence, and rewrite it on the line below.
wood it be inpossible to live in modern times without computers

_____

3 Which word is **not** a synonym for *helpful*?
Ⓐ effective   Ⓑ cooperative   Ⓒ destructive   Ⓓ useful

4 Revise the sentence below.
She was trying to think of a good invention that could help her finished her chores.

_____

5 Which sentence is out of order?
¹**Lisa was getting ready for the party.** ²**Then, she put the cupcakes in a container.**
³**She was almost ready to leave.** ⁴**First, she wrapped the video game she was giving her best friend.**
Ⓐ 1   Ⓑ 2   Ⓒ 3   Ⓓ 4

6 "Some inventions are just new ways to use common materials." Which detail below would **not** support this topic sentence?
Ⓐ Star-shaped ice cube trays were invented as a fun twist to the common trays.
Ⓑ The person who invented the portable television had the creative idea of carrying a TV anywhere he went.
Ⓒ Some day a person might invent a rocket ship that can take people to other solar systems.
Ⓓ Tennis shoes that used Velcro instead of laces were created to help children who had trouble tying their shoes.

PREWRITE
Turn this paper over, and draw five boxes. In each box, list one idea for an invention. It could be a new idea or a creative twist on something that's already invented.

QUICKWRITE
Give me five! What are five creative ideas you have for new inventions? Which one do you think would be most popular? Explain why.

Writing Warm-up 42

1 Underline any nouns and circle any pronouns in the sentence below.
Would you like to go on the train to the zoo with us this weekend?

2 Edit the following sentence, and rewrite it on the line below.
i think its the prettyest garden that ive ever scene in a city

_____

3 Which word is **not** a synonym for *necessary*?
Ⓐ wanted
Ⓑ needed
Ⓒ required
Ⓓ vital

4 Revise the sentence below.
Why did she dreamed that shes couldn't lived without her watch?

_____

5 Which sentence is out of order?
¹**What a fun and memorable vacation! ²Sarah was ready to pack for her first vacation away from home. ³Once she was packed, she left for the airport. ⁴The plane landed in Tahiti.**
Ⓐ 1   Ⓑ 2   Ⓒ 3   Ⓓ 4

6 "I have many things to donate to charity." Which detail below would **not** support this topic sentence?
Ⓐ These two bags of clothes will be useful to someone.
Ⓑ Charities are organized to collect money and items for people in need.
Ⓒ The couch and chair will be given to the organization.
Ⓓ This new computer works so well that these old ones can go to charity.

PREWRITE
Turn this paper over, and draw five boxes. In each box, list one thing you own that you couldn't live without.

QUICKWRITE
Give me five! What are five personal possessions that you couldn't live without. Explain the importance of each one.

Daily Writing Warm-ups 3–4 © 2006 Creative Teaching Press

Writing Warm-up 43

1 Underline any nouns and circle any pronouns in the sentence below.
Do you remember where we put our emergency earthquake kits?

2 Edit the following sentence, and rewrite it on the line below.
she couldnt find the flashlights candles or radio in all the confushion

_____

3 Which word is **not** a synonym for *safe*?
Ⓐ dangerous   Ⓑ protected   Ⓒ secure   Ⓓ harmless

4 Revise the sentence below.
She feeled safe with hers family even though the house was dark and scary.

_____

5 Which sentences should be switched?
¹**Suddenly, the house started shaking.** ²**The Guzman family was enjoying a game in the living room after dinner.** ³**Michelle began to cry, because she was so startled.** ⁴**Mr. Guzman tried to calm her down.**
Ⓐ 1 and 2   Ⓑ 1 and 3   Ⓒ 1 and 4   Ⓓ 2 and 4

6 "Prepare for an earthquake by putting together a kit that includes safety equipment."
Which detail below would **not** support this topic sentence?
Ⓐ It is important to keep food in the kit.
Ⓑ A flashlight will help you find your way at night if the lights go out.
Ⓒ A package of bandages can help if something falls and you get a cut.
Ⓓ A radio will warn you of emergency procedures and when to evacuate.

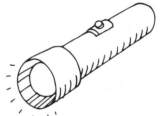

PREWRITE Turn this paper over, and draw five boxes. In each box, list one thing you think is important to include in an emergency kit.

QUICKWRITE Give me five! What are five things that every emergency kit should include? Explain the usefulness of each item.

Writing Warm-up 44

1 Underline any nouns and circle any pronouns in the sentence below.
Hannah loves her name because it is spelled the same forward and backward.

2 Edit the following sentence, and rewrite it on the line below.
can you think of sombody who has a name you simply love

_____

3 Which word is **not** a synonym for *pretty* as in "a *pretty* name"?
    Ⓐ cute   Ⓑ winning   Ⓒ beautiful   Ⓓ lovely

4 Revise the sentence below.
He dreamded that he had forgot his name on the first day of school!

_____

5 Which sentences should be switched?
¹Parents spend a great deal of time trying to pick out the best name for their children. ²Some children are named after relatives. ³Parents often spend months selecting a name. ⁴Some children are even named after their parents.

    Ⓐ 1 and 2
    Ⓑ 2 and 3
    Ⓒ 3 and 4
    Ⓓ 1 and 4

6 "Some names are quite uncommon in North America." Which detail below would **not** support this topic sentence?
    Ⓐ Many children share the names John and Jessica.
    Ⓑ One rare name for a boy is Gunther.
    Ⓒ There are very few children named Shiloh, although it's a beautiful name.
    Ⓓ Another name that you don't hear very often is Teisha.

PREWRITE
Turn this paper over, and draw eight boxes. In each box, list one name you like that matches your gender.

QUICKWRITE
Give me five! What are five names that you would like to use some day for a pet, a child, or a character in a story? Why do you like each name?

Daily Writing Warm-ups 3–4 © 2006 Creative Teaching Press

Writing Warm-up 45

1 Underline any nouns and circle any pronouns in the sentence below.
You can meet an author at your nearest bookstore this weekend.

2 Edit the following sentence, and rewrite it on the line below.
**did you meat that famous football playr win he came to
our school**

_____

3 Which word is **not** a synonym for *happy*?
    Ⓐ dissatisfied   Ⓑ pleased   Ⓒ glad   Ⓓ joyful

4 Revise the sentence below.
She forgotted that she shouldn't shined the light right into the actor's face.

_____

5 Which sentence is out of order?
¹Dr. Jane Goodall spoke at the fund-raiser about the importance of protecting chimps. ²The winner paid $3,000 for the photographs. ³There was an auction of enlarged photographs by the famed Howard Buffet. ⁴The money raised from the auction would be used to improve the lives of the chimps living wild in Ghana.
    Ⓐ 1   Ⓑ 2   Ⓒ 3   Ⓓ 4

6 "People can become famous for many different reasons." Which detail below would **not** support this topic sentence?
    Ⓐ Jack Wagner is a famous actor on television.
    Ⓑ Some people become famous because they are talented piano players or singers.
    Ⓒ Many doctors have become quite famous after developing cures or vaccines for diseases.
    Ⓓ Many people have become famous and wealthy through hard work and education.

PREWRITE Turn this paper over, and draw five boxes. In each box, list one famous person. Try to think of people who are famous for different reasons.

QUICKWRITE Give me five! Who are five people you would love to meet? Why do you want to meet them? What would you say?

Name_____ Date _____

QUIZ 5

1 Underline any nouns and circle any pronouns in the sentence below.
Do you have any idea where he put the folder that has our comic strips?

2 Edit the following sentence, and rewrite it on the line below.
it was hard for evrybody to agree on a knew design for the school calander

_____

3 Which word is **not** a synonym for _icky_?
Ⓐ gross
Ⓑ disgusting
Ⓒ tasty
Ⓓ yucky

4 Revise the sentence below.
She feeled so tired after helping her sister that she sat down to rest.

_____

5 Which sentence is out of order?
¹Stacey felt sick. ²The thermometer read 102 degrees. ³Within ten minutes, she was at the doctor's office. ⁴Her older brother took her temperature to see if she had a fever.

Ⓐ 1   Ⓑ 2   Ⓒ 3   Ⓓ 4

6 "Gardeners do many tasks in the yard." Which detail below would **not** support this topic sentence?
Ⓐ Gardeners work long, hard days.
Ⓑ They mow the lawn and trim the hedges.
Ⓒ Many gardeners plant flowers and trim trees.
Ⓓ In many cases, gardeners will remove weeds and plant new grass.

Give your best effort!

Daily Writing Warm-ups 3–4 © 2006 Creative Teaching Press

Writing Warm-up 46

1 Underline any adjectives in the sentence below.
The friends thought the movie was sad but realistic.

2 Edit the following sentence, and rewrite it on the line below.
would you buy popcorn candy and a hot dog at the movies

_____

3 Which word is a synonym for *funny* as in "a *funny* comedy"?
    Ⓐ strange   Ⓑ somber   Ⓒ humorous   Ⓓ cute

4 Revise the sentence below.
She thought the movie was so funny that she almost choked on her popcorn.

_____

5 Which sentence is out of order?
[1]**They wondered if there would be a sequel, since the ending left them hanging.**
[2]**The movie was about to begin.** [3]**They sat and enjoyed the entire movie without even screaming once!** [4]**Well, they did scream near the end of the movie.**
    Ⓐ 1   Ⓑ 2   Ⓒ 3   Ⓓ 4

6 "There are companies that will deliver any DVD you want for a flat fee each month." Which detail below best supports this topic sentence?
    Ⓐ Movie theaters offer matinee prices, which are a bit cheaper if you are willing to go during the day.
    Ⓑ You can subscribe to a service that will deliver movies to your mailbox.
    Ⓒ Some people prefer going to the theater, because they enjoy watching movies on a big screen.
    Ⓓ By renting a DVD movie, you can sit in the comfort of your own home watching movies in your pajamas.

PREWRITE Turn this paper over, and draw a line down the middle. Write *Movie Theater* on the left and *DVD* on the right. List three benefits and three drawbacks of each one.

QUICKWRITE Movie theaters or DVDs? How do you prefer to watch movies? Justify your choice using BOTH benefits and drawbacks.

Writing Warm-up 47

1 Underline any adjectives in the sentence below.
Snacking throughout the day can be part of a healthy lifestyle.

2 Edit the following sentence, and rewrite it on the line below.
she decided to by a calander to list the sweet salty and crunchy snacks she ate each day

_____

3 Which word is a synonym for _healthy_ as in "_healthy_ snacking"?
     Ⓐ clever   Ⓑ smart   Ⓒ delicious   Ⓓ ongoing

4 Revise the sentence below.
He packed some healthy snacks to eaten at recess.

_____

5 Which sentences should be switched?
¹The apples were ripe and ready to be picked. ²The crates were collected in trucks and transported to the grocery stores. ³The workers picked every apple and packed them in crates. ⁴Families could then buy the apples from the store.
     Ⓐ 1 and 2   Ⓑ 2 and 3   Ⓒ 1 and 3   Ⓓ 2 and 4

6 "Homemade chocolate chip cookies make delicious snacks." Which detail below best supports this topic sentence?
     Ⓐ There's nothing better than homemade chocolate chip cookies.
     Ⓑ Snacking on one or two chocolate chip cookies can be a smart choice.
     Ⓒ The sweet flavor of chocolate chip cookies makes them a popular snack.
     Ⓓ Many people would rather have fruit than chocolate chip cookies.

PREWRITE
Turn this paper over, and draw a line down the middle. Write _Cookies_ on the left and _Fruits_ on the right. List three benefits and three drawbacks of each snack.

QUICKWRITE
Cookies or fruit? Which do you prefer as a snack? Justify your choice using BOTH benefits and drawbacks.

Daily Writing Warm-ups 3–4 © 2006 Creative Teaching Press

Writing Warm-up 48

1 Underline any adjectives in the sentence below.
Have you seen the fluffy, yellow dog that she adopted from the animal shelter?

2 Edit the following sentence, and rewrite it on the line below.
there were severall cats dogs and rabbits at the animal shelter

_____

3 Which word is a synonym for *cute* as in "a *cute* puppy"?
Ⓐ beautiful   Ⓑ adorable   © cuddly   Ⓓ frightful

4 Revise the sentence below.
They had forgotted that the cute kitten couldn't be adopted until it was eight weeks old.

_____

5 Which sentence is out of order?
**¹Joe decided to call a mobile dog groomer to come to his house to wash his dog.
²The dog groomer showed up, carried the dog to his trailer, and bathed Joe's dog.
³Joe's dog looked so fluffy and clean when he came out of the grooming trailer! ⁴The dog groomer at the pet store was so busy that Joe couldn't could get an appointment.**
Ⓐ 1   Ⓑ 2   © 3   Ⓓ 4

6 "Dogs make better pets than cats." Which detail below best supports this topic sentence?
Ⓐ Cats love to cuddle on your lap while you watch television.
Ⓑ Dogs enjoy going on walks at least once a day.
© Cats are easier to carry than many dogs.
Ⓓ Dogs enjoy spending time with families, but many cats are happy roaming alone.

PREWRITE Turn this paper over, and draw a line down the middle. Write *Dogs* on the left and *Cats* on the right. List three benefits and three drawbacks of each pet.

QUICKWRITE Dogs or cats? Which do you prefer as a pet? Justify your choice using BOTH benefits and drawbacks.

Writing Warm-up 49

1 Underline any adjectives in the sentence below.
Sports cars are fast on the road, but SUVs carry more passengers.

2 Edit the following sentence, and rewrite it on the line below.
she went to the doctor dentist and car dealership with her family

_____

3 Which word is a synonym for *fast* as in "a *fast* car"?
Ⓐ speedy   Ⓑ cool   Ⓒ sporty   Ⓓ expensive

4 Revise the sentence below.
He forget to make an appointment to test drive the fast, new sports car.

_____

5 Which sentence is out of order?
¹The brochure finally came in the mail. ²He'd been waiting three months to read the details of the new SUV. ³He wanted to know everything possible about the vehicle before going to the dealership. ⁴After seeing the commercial, he ordered a copy of the sales brochure for the SUV.

Ⓐ 1   Ⓑ 2   Ⓒ 3   Ⓓ 4

6 "SUVs are safer than sports cars." Which detail below best supports this topic sentence?
Ⓐ Sports cars can reach faster speeds in a shorter amount of time than SUVs.
Ⓑ Large families often prefer SUVs because there is enough space for everyone to ride together.
Ⓒ Many SUVs weigh so much more than sports cars that they can hold up in a crash better than smaller cars.
Ⓓ Families often choose SUVs since they can fit sporting goods and children in the back seats.

PREWRITE Turn this paper over, and draw a line down the middle. Write *SUVs* on the left and *Sports Cars* on the right. List three benefits and three drawbacks of each vehicle.

QUICKWRITE SUV or sports car? Which do you prefer as a family vehicle? Justify your choice using BOTH benefits and drawbacks.

Writing Warm-up 50

1 Underline any adjectives in the sentence below.
She was such an intelligent and responsible student that she won many awards in school.

2 Edit the following sentence, and rewrite it on the line below.
mr jones had such an increedible class that he smiled all the thyme

_____

3 Which word is a synonym for _good_ as in "a _good_ student"?
Ⓐ fantastic   Ⓑ nice   Ⓒ rebellious   Ⓓ leader

4 Revise the sentence below.
What do you think it taked to be a good student every year in school?

_____

5 Which sentence is out of order?
¹She made a plan to improve her scores for her father. ²She would do her homework every night as soon as she got home. ³She would also make note cards to help her practice the information she found difficult to remember. ⁴Her father said that if she got higher grades, then he would allow her to play soccer.
Ⓐ 1   Ⓑ 2   Ⓒ 3   Ⓓ 4

6 "To be successful in school, a person needs to make studying a priority." Which detail below best supports this topic sentence?
Ⓐ She thought that playing with her friends was more important than homework.
Ⓑ Although playing is important to growth and development, students need to focus on schoolwork first.
Ⓒ Some successful students have different strategies for learning new material.
Ⓓ If teachers gave less homework, then students would have more time to play.

PREWRITE Turn this paper over, and draw a line down the middle. Write _Teachers_ on the left and _Students_ on the right. List three benefits and three drawbacks of each role.

QUICKWRITE Teacher or student? Which role would you prefer? Justify your choice using BOTH benefits and drawbacks.

Writing Warm-up 51

1 Underline any adjectives in the sentence below.
She lived in a large, roomy apartment in a crowded city.

2 Edit the following sentence, and rewrite it on the line below.
the large home in yountville was a reel barginn compared to the small expensive home in the city

_____

3 Which word is a synonym for _big_ as in "a _big_ house"?
   Ⓐ spacious   Ⓑ awesome   Ⓒ petite   Ⓓ biggest

4 Revise the sentence below.
Her room was so big that it could fitted a king-size bed and two dressers!

_____

5 Which sentence is out of order?
**¹The realtor made a list of 20 homes for them to view.
²They looked at every home to find just the right one.
³The Olsons wanted to move to the country, so they hired a realtor to find them a home. ⁴Finally, they found the perfect home.**

   Ⓐ 1   Ⓑ 2   Ⓒ 3   Ⓓ 4

6 "The new building trend called 'urban living' creates lofts and condos above businesses."
Which detail below best supports this topic sentence?
   Ⓐ The four levels of lofts and condos were built above a coffee house, a bank, and a small grocery store.
   Ⓑ Urban living was created with the idea that people could walk to everything they needed.
   Ⓒ Would you be interested in buying a condo above a donut shop?
   Ⓓ Some builders have made a great deal of money by building up rather than out, since it takes up less land.

PREWRITE Turn this paper over, and draw a line down the middle. Write _City_ on the left and _Country_ on the right. List three benefits and three drawbacks of each one.

QUICKWRITE City or country? Where would you prefer to live? Justify your choice using BOTH benefits and drawbacks.

Writing Warm-up 52

1 Underline any adjectives in the sentence below.
As a young child, Sam knew he wanted to become an astronomer because he was fascinated with the sparkly stars in the night sky.

2 Edit the following sentence, and rewrite it on the line below.
she loves to count the stars look for planets and watch the moon at night

_____

_____

3 Which word is a synonym for *nice* as in "a *nice* day"?
Ⓐ sweet   Ⓑ kind   Ⓒ pleasant   Ⓓ uneventful

4 Revise the sentence below.
On Tori's way outta the door, her mother said, "Have a nice day."

_____

_____

5 Which sentences should be switched?
¹Once on the road, they discussed which water rides they wanted to go on first. ²The Phillips family was planning a day trip to the nearby water park. ³Each brother got to pick three water rides. ⁴Luckily, every ride they chose was open that day.
Ⓐ 1 and 3   Ⓑ 1 and 2   Ⓒ 2 and 3   Ⓓ 3 and 4

6 "College classes are offered during the day and at night to allow students choice and flexibility." Which detail below best supports this topic sentence?
Ⓐ Some students choose to take college classes at night.
Ⓑ A college education is important for every person in today's society.
Ⓒ Since some students work during the day, the college offers night classes.
Ⓓ Day classes are often less crowded than night classes.

PREWRITE Turn this paper over, and draw a line down the middle. Write *Day* on the left and *Night* on the right. List three benefits and three drawbacks of each one.

QUICKWRITE Day or night? During which time of the day do you feel most alert and happy? Which do you prefer? Justify your choice using BOTH benefits and drawbacks.

Writing Warm-up 53

1 Underline any adjectives in the sentence below.
Would you rather have a slice of hot pizza or do you prefer cold pizza?

2 Edit the following sentence, and rewrite it on the line below.
they had allready waited over an our for the pizza delivery to arrive

_____

3 Which word is a synonym for _called_ as in "_called_ the Mega Meaty Pizza"?
Ⓐ phoned   Ⓑ asked   Ⓒ named   Ⓓ titled

4 Revise the sentence below.
Her funny friends called her "Pizza Queen," since she always made the best pizza!

_____

5 Which sentence is out of order?
¹Linda brought her homemade pizza to the dining-room table. ²In the end, everyone agreed it was the best they had ever tasted. ³Each person ate at least two slices of her amazing creation. ⁴There were so many toppings, that it pleased everyone.
Ⓐ 1   Ⓑ 2   Ⓒ 3   Ⓓ 4

6 "There are many types of vegetables that make great pizza toppings." Which detail below best supports this topic sentence?
Ⓐ Baked potatoes are popular side dishes, since they are healthy and flavorful.
Ⓑ Pepperoni and sausage are the most popular pizza toppings.
Ⓒ Onions can be grilled, baked, or eaten raw.
Ⓓ Green peppers, olives, and fresh Roma tomatoes are popular pizza toppings.

PREWRITE Turn this paper over, and draw a line down the middle. Write _Homemade Pizza_ on the left and _Delivery Pizza_ on the right. List three benefits and three drawbacks of each pizza.

QUICKWRITE Homemade pizza or delivery pizza? Which do you prefer? Justify your choice using BOTH benefits and drawbacks.

Daily Writing Warm-ups 3–4 © 2006 Creative Teaching Press

Writing Warm-up 54

1 Underline any adjectives in the sentence below.
Last summer, Sam took a vacation to the beautiful, spacious state of Alaska.

2 Edit the following sentence, and rewrite it on the line below.
do you notice the sent of freshly cooked salmon coming from that restaurant

_____

3 Which word is a synonym for *usual* as in "just a *usual* day"?
 Ⓐ unusual Ⓑ boring Ⓒ fun Ⓓ ordinary

4 Revise the sentence below.
On a typical summer day, you will find the boys swimmed in their backyard pool.

_____

5 Which sentence is out of order?
¹In the fall months, squirrels gather nuts and acorns. ²This instinct is the key to their survival. ³They hide the nuts and acorns in secret storage locations, which they later revisit. ⁴They know that they need to store food for the cold winter ahead.
 Ⓐ 1 Ⓑ 2 Ⓒ 3 Ⓓ 4

6 "Some sports can be enjoyed in both winter and summer." Which detail below best supports this topic sentence?

 Ⓐ Skiing is a popular winter sport in many areas of the world.
 Ⓑ Soccer, football, and tennis can be played in any season because there are indoor courts and arenas.
 Ⓒ One popular summer game is beach volleyball.
 Ⓓ Swimming in rivers and lakes is popular in many locations of the world.

PREWRITE Turn this paper over, and draw a line down the middle. Write *Winter* on the left and *Summer* on the right. List three benefits and three drawbacks of each season.

QUICKWRITE Winter or summer? Which do you prefer? Justify your choice using BOTH benefits and drawbacks.

QUIZ 6

1 Underline any adjectives in the sentence below.
What do you call those tiny, colorful flowers that you planted in your backyard garden?

2 Edit the following sentence, and rewrite it on the line below.
the sight of dr. ann's knew office had been choosen

_____

3 Which word or phrase is a synonym for *real* as in "that is the *real* answer"?
    Ⓐ made-up   Ⓑ false   Ⓒ meaningful   Ⓓ true

4 Revise the sentence below.
She forgotted to do her homeworks, so she dreams she had to stay after school.

_____

_____

5 Which sentences should be switched?
¹The carpets were getting so filthy that Keith decided to clean them. ²He took out the professional carpet cleaner and filled it with cleaning solution. ³Within three hours, the carpets looked and smelled much cleaner. ⁴He pushed the machine back and forth over every inch of the carpet.
    Ⓐ 1 and 2
    Ⓑ 2 and 3
    Ⓒ 1 and 4
    Ⓓ 3 and 4

6 "Gates left open are a common reason why some dogs get lost." Which detail below best supports this topic sentence?
    Ⓐ People need to remember to lock their gates, since dogs often wander out.
    Ⓑ If you are a good neighbor, then you would return a lost dog as soon as possible.
    Ⓒ People need to check their gates to make sure they are always locked.
    Ⓓ It's dangerous for a dog to wander the streets in any neighborhood.

Show what you know!

SCORE

Writing Warm-up 55

1 Underline any nouns and circle any adjectives in the sentence below.
Are you coming to my birthday party at the skating rink this weekend?

2 Edit the following sentence, and rewrite it on the line below.
who wood you name as your closest kindest and most thoughtful friend

_____

3 Write three synonyms for the word *nice* as in "a *nice* friend."

_____   _____   _____

4 Revise the sentence below.
Do you think youself are a good friend to others?

_____

5 Which is the best sequence for these sentences?
**¹People become friends in many different ways. ²Sometimes
they live near each other, so they play together often. ³In
other cases, they meet after discovering that they have
something in common. ⁴That's usually when they develop
a deep friendship.**

Ⓐ 1-2-3-4   Ⓑ 2-1-4-3   Ⓒ 4-1-2-3   Ⓓ 1-2-4-3

6 Choose the sentence below that gives your own opinion and supports this statement:
Friends will always support you in time of need.
Ⓐ Friends will listen when you feel frustrated or sad.
Ⓑ A true friend will offer advice only when you ask for it.
Ⓒ I think friendship means that sometimes you give in instead of expecting to
always get your way.
Ⓓ If you ask me, friends will always offer a hug, smile, or kind word just when you
need it.

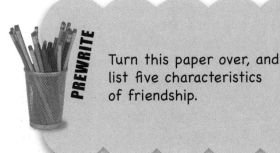
PREWRITE Turn this paper over, and list five characteristics of friendship.

QUICKWRITE You received an anonymous letter saying, "How do you make friends?" Write an advice column in response. Give your opinions and advice to this person.

Name_____   Date _____

Writing Warm-up 56

1 Underline any nouns and circle any adjectives in the sentence below.
As a respectful child, you should always do what your loving parents ask you to do.

2 Edit the following sentence, and rewrite it on the line below.
why is that big green grasshopper on your sealing

_____

3 Write three synonyms for the word *tell* as in "*tell* them."

_____   _____   _____

4 Revise the sentence below.
It's a fact of live that you don't always get to do what you wanted to do.

_____

5 Which is the best sequence for these sentences?
¹The construction crew showed up around 9:00. ²By noon, the carpet was ripped out. ³By the late afternoon, the first tiles were on the floor. ⁴The day for new flooring had arrived.

    Ⓐ 1-2-3-4   Ⓑ 2-1-4-3   Ⓒ 4-1-2-3   Ⓓ 1-2-4-3

6 Choose the sentence below that gives your own opinion and supports this statement:
Being a child means respecting your parents and realizing that they sometimes make choices for you.
    Ⓐ You should always respect what your parents say.
    Ⓑ Parents have experienced more things that help them to know what is best for you.
    Ⓒ I think that parents always know what is best for you, so you should do what they ask.
    Ⓓ In my opinion, children should have more control over their decision-making.

PREWRITE
Turn this paper over, and list five reasons why parents deserve your respect.

QUICKWRITE
You received an anonymous letter saying, "How do I get out of doing something my parents have asked me to do?" Write an advice column in response. Give your opinions and advice to this person.

Writing Warm-up 57

1 Underline any nouns and circle any adjectives in the sentence below.
Are you really going to the beautiful, tropical island of Hawaii in December?

2 Edit the following sentence, and rewrite it on the line below.
are you visiting the museum tropical gardens and ancient ruins while in mexico

_____

3 Write three synonyms for the word *good* as in "a *good* vacation."

_____   _____   _____

4 Revise the sentence below.
Did I telled you what a good vacation I had last year in Africa?

_____

5 Which is the best sequence for these sentences?
¹The truck was packed with sleeping bags, suitcases, and tents. ²The Rish family was going on a camping trip ³After nine long hours of driving, they arrived at the national park. ⁴They pitched their tents and set up camp.

Ⓐ 1-2-3-4   Ⓑ 2-1-4-3   Ⓒ 4-1-2-3   Ⓓ 2-1-3-4

6 Choose the sentence below that gives your own opinion and supports this statement:
Warm, tropical places are the best destinations for family vacations.
    Ⓐ If your family likes to ski, then the best vacation spot is either Utah or Colorado.
    Ⓑ Hawaii is warm and tropical, so it makes a great vacation spot.
    Ⓒ Tropical places allow families more activity choices than cold-weather locations.
    Ⓓ Vacationing with your family helps you bond just like my family did on our last trip to Hawaii.

PREWRITE
Turn this paper over, and list five characteristics of a fun family vacation.

QUICKWRITE
You received an anonymous letter saying, "How do I have the most fun on my family vacation this summer?" Write an advice column in response. Give your opinions and advice to this person.

Name_____   Date _____

Writing Warm-up 58

1 Underline any nouns and circle any adjectives in the sentence below.
By taking chewable vitamins every morning, Katie will grow up to be a strong and healthy girl.

2 Edit the following sentence, and rewrite it on the line below.
do you no that evrybody needs to take better care of there teeth skin and bones

_____

3 Write three synonyms for the word *smart* as in "*smart* choices."

_____   _____   _____

4 Revise the sentence below.
He rised when the presenter said, "Please stand up if yous drinks at least one glass of milk every day."

_____

5 Which is the best sequence for these sentences?
[1]**She made everyone promise to chew the gum only with parental permission.** [2]**Each bag contained a toothbrush, floss, and sugarless gum.** [3]**She brought goody bags for each student.** [4]**During Dental Awareness Month, the local dentist, Dr. Yaryan, visited the school.**

Ⓐ 4-3-2-1   Ⓑ 2-1-4-3   Ⓒ 4-1-2-3   Ⓓ 2-1-3-4

6 Choose the sentence below that gives your own opinion and supports this statement:
Eating balanced meals is part of a healthy diet.

Ⓐ I think that when people eat too much of one item, they don't feel well because they are not eating a balanced diet.
Ⓑ A balanced meal means eating protein, vegetables, and fruits.
Ⓒ Eating well will affect your future health.
Ⓓ I don't think eating a balanced meal is really that important.

PREWRITE
Turn this paper over, and list five characteristics of a healthy lifestyle.

QUICKWRITE
You received an anonymous letter saying, "How do I grow up to be healthy and strong?" Write an advice column in response. Give your opinions and advice to this person.

Daily Writing Warm-ups 3–4 © 2006 Creative Teaching Press

Writing Warm-up 59

1 Underline any nouns and circle any adjectives in the sentence below.
Some people do unpleasant chores for others to earn extra money.

2 Edit the following sentence, and rewrite it on the line below.
julie stoped shopping on the Internet when she realized she was spending to much money

_____

3 Write three synonyms for the word *bad* as in *"bad* spending."

_____   _____   _____

4 Revise the sentence below.
It's a good thing she didn't waste her money on the video game player, because a gooder one is coming out soon.

_____

5 Which is the best sequence for these sentences?
¹**Molly decided to put all of it in a bank account to earn interest until she was older.** ²**That way she might have a good college savings fund.** ³**Molly received a total of $120 for her birthday.** ⁴**Her mother suggested she either put it in a bank account or a savings bond.**
Ⓐ 3-4-1-2   Ⓑ 2-1-4-3   Ⓒ 4-1-2-3   Ⓓ 3-1-2-4

6 Choose the sentence below that gives your own opinion and supports this statement:
Saving money is always better than spending it on something you won't use very often.
Ⓐ A lot of money is wasted on toys children only play with once.
Ⓑ I think you should consider how often you will play with a toy before deciding to buy it.
Ⓒ In my opinion, children have too many expensive toys.
Ⓓ I'd have to say that saving money will teach you good habits in patience.

PREWRITE
Turn this paper over, and list five smart ways to earn and save money.

QUICKWRITE
You received an anonymous letter saying, "How can I save money for college?" Write an advice column in response. Give your opinions and advice to this person.

Writing Warm-up 60

1 Underline any nouns and circle any adjectives in the sentence below.
A submarine sandwich often has fresh lettuce and tomato.

2 Edit the following sentence, and rewrite it on the line below.
police officer williams was the first person on the seen after the alarm sounded

_____

3 Write three synonyms for the word *yummy* as in "a *yummy* sandwich."

_____   _____   _____

4 Revise the sentence below.
The sandwich he ordering tasted so bad that he tooken it right back to the shop.

_____

5 Which is the best sequence for these sentences?
¹He gave the sales clerk a coupon that read "buy one – get one free." ²Mike walked into the shop with $5.00. ³The sign behind the counter said that Mike's favorite sandwich would cost $3.99. ⁴Mike walked out with two sandwiches!

Ⓐ 3-4-1-2   Ⓑ 2-3-1-4   Ⓒ 4-1-2-3   Ⓓ 3-1-2-4

6 Choose the sentence below that gives your own opinion and supports this statement:
There are at least 20 different variations of the submarine sandwich based on the ingredients.

Ⓐ There are so many ingredients that you can end up with many different sandwiches.
Ⓑ My favorite is the Italian submarine sandwich with ham, salami, and cheese.
Ⓒ You should look at all the choices before ordering, since there are so many sandwiches that can be made.
Ⓓ If you're asking me, you should get a submarine sandwich for lunch.

PREWRITE
Turn this paper over, and list five items you think should be on a submarine sandwich.

QUICKWRITE
You received an anonymous letter saying, "How do I make the tastiest submarine sandwich?" Write an advice column in response. Give your opinions and advice to this person.

Daily Writing Warm-ups 3–4 © 2006 Creative Teaching Press

Name_____   Date _____

Writing Warm-up 61

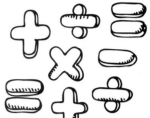

1 Underline any nouns and circle any adjectives in the sentence below.
Math skills will be necessary in every job you will ever have.

2 Edit the following sentence, and rewrite it on the line below.
its amazeing how you solved that problem without using your fingers a calculator or a pencil and paper

_____

_____

3 Write three synonyms for the word *hard* as in "a *hard* problem."

_____   _____   _____

4 Revise the sentence below.
She was such a smart student that she could solve hard math problems in she's head.

_____

5 Which is the best sequence for these sentences?
¹The problems began flashing on the computer screen. ²Every student was focused and ready to go. ³The Mental Math-a-thon was about to begin. ⁴The winner of the contest received the Math Medal.

    Ⓐ 3-4-1-2   Ⓑ 3-2-1-4   Ⓒ 4-1-2-3   Ⓓ 3-1-2-4

6 Choose the sentence below that gives your own opinion and supports this statement:
Mechanics, doctors, and airline pilots are three examples of workers who use math every day.

    Ⓐ Airline pilots must use math to calculate how far they are from other planes, so I think that's an important reason to be good in math.
    Ⓑ Mechanics fix cars, measure oil amounts, and calculate speeds.
    Ⓒ Doctors are very important workers, if you ask me, because they save lives.
    Ⓓ In my opinion, airline pilots should make more money.

Daily Writing Warm-ups 3–4 © 2006 Creative Teaching Press

PREWRITE
Turn this paper over, and list five ways to get better in math.

QUICKWRITE
You received an anonymous letter saying, "How can I improve my math grade?" Write an advice column in response. Give your opinions and advice to this person.

Writing Warm-up **62**

1 Underline any nouns and circle any adjectives in the sentence below.
Professional photographers spend years learning how to take clear photos that focus on colorful images.

2 Edit the following sentence, and rewrite it on the line below.
did you sea the article in wensedays paper describing the upcoming photo contest

_____

3 Write three synonyms for the word *some* as in "took *some* photos."

_____   _____   _____

4 Revise the sentence below.
She falled off the log trying to tooken pictures of the baby bird slept in the nest.

_____

5 Which is the best sequence for these sentences?
¹First, take some photos with a digital camera. ²Then, connect it to a computer and upload the photos into a program. ³It's easy to print your own pictures. ⁴Before you know it, they are ready to print.

Ⓐ 1-2-4-3   Ⓑ 3-1-2-4   Ⓒ 4-1-2-3   Ⓓ 2-1-4-3

6 Choose the sentence below that gives your own opinion and supports this statement:
These days anyone can take quality pictures like a professional photographer.

Ⓐ I think if you have a good digital camera, you can take great pictures.
Ⓑ If you ask me, digital cameras are still too expensive.
Ⓒ In my opinion, anyone with a camera can be a photographer.
Ⓓ I think that you should go out and buy a digital camera.

PREWRITE
Turn this paper over, and list five things you know about taking photographs.

QUICKWRITE

You received an anonymous letter saying, "How can I take better pictures with my new camera?" Write an advice column in response. Give your opinions and advice to this person.

Daily Writing Warm-ups 3–4 © 2006 Creative Teaching Press

Writing Warm-up 63

1 Underline any nouns and circle any adjectives in the sentence below.
She quit her job to dedicate all of her time to raising money for the wild chimpanzees in Africa.

2 Edit the following sentence, and rewrite it on the line below.
is the auction going to be on teusday or wedesday of next weak

_____

3 Write three synonyms for the words *a lot* as in "raise *a lot* of money."

_____   _____   _____

4 Revise the sentence below.
John readed the brochure while he waiting for the program to begin.

_____

5 Which is the best sequence for these sentences?
¹Later, the goat could have baby goats, which could be sold for more money. ²The goat would provide the family with fresh milk and cheese, which they could not afford otherwise. ³The card said that a goat was donated in her name to a poor family in Peru. ⁴For her birthday, Kelly received an interesting card.

   Ⓐ 3-4-1-2   Ⓑ 4-1-2-3   Ⓒ 4-3-2-1   Ⓓ 2-1-4-3

6 Choose the sentence below that gives your own opinion and supports this statement: **Every year millions of people donate money to charities that are dedicated to helping others.**

   Ⓐ I think that everyone should donate at least one dollar a year to a charity.
   Ⓑ The purpose of a charity is to gather money and give it to those most in need.
   Ⓒ The many people who donate each year are doing acts of kindness.
   Ⓓ You can donate money to a variety of charities.

PREWRITE Turn this paper over, and list five ways to raise money.

QUICKWRITE You received an anonymous letter saying, "How can I raise some money for the nearby animal shelter?" Write an advice column in response. Give your opinions and advice to this person.

Name_____ Date _____

1 Underline any nouns and circle any adjectives in the sentence below.
Her raspberry hot chocolate was served without whipped cream or chocolate sprinkles.

2 Edit the following sentence, and rewrite it on the line below.
didnt you think the first seen of the play was amazeing

_____

3 Write three synonyms for the word *good* as in *"good* ideas."

_____   _____   _____

4 Revise the sentence below.
The good ice-cream sandwich was melting all on her clothes.

_____

5 Which is the best sequence for these sentences?
¹The parade was coming around the corner. ²Everyone sat along the parade route waiting to see the marching bands and floats. ³As the first float appeared, everyone cheered and applauded. ⁴Then we heard the local high school band.
- Ⓐ 2-1-3-4
- Ⓑ 1-2-3-4
- Ⓒ 4-3-2-1
- Ⓓ 2-3-1-4

6 "Rabbits make loving and cuddly pets." Which supporting sentence most clearly shows that you are giving your own opinion?
- Ⓐ I think rabbits are better than dogs or cats.
- Ⓑ If you ask me, seeing a rabbit fall asleep in your arms is priceless.
- Ⓒ Have you ever held a soft, furry rabbit?
- Ⓓ Rabbits enjoy nibbling on grass, dandelion greens, and spinach.

Give it your all!

SCORE

80

Daily Writing Warm-ups 3–4 © 2006 Creative Teaching Press

Writing Warm-up 64

1 Underline any adverbs in the sentence below.
The puppy chewed quietly on his new squeaky toy in the corner of the living room.

2 Edit the following sentence, and rewrite it on the line below.
did he like the squeaky bone the stuffed animal or the tennis ball the best

_____

3 Write three synonyms for the word *idea*.

_____   _____   _____

4 Revise the sentence below.
That silly dog thinked it was so fun to runned around the house with a shoe in its mouth.

_____

5 Which is the best sequence for these sentences?
¹Susan wanted to build her puppy a doghouse. ²First, she bought the materials at the local hardware store. ³Once the materials were organized, she read the directions. ⁴Within hours, there was a new doghouse in her backyard.

Ⓐ 1-2-3-4   Ⓑ 4-2-3-1   Ⓒ 1-4-2-3   Ⓓ 3-2-1-4

6 Which sentence is most likely told from the dog's point of view?
Ⓐ It was hard building the doghouse, but it was worth it.
Ⓑ I don't want to sleep in that scary doghouse when I can sleep in your cozy house.
Ⓒ The supplies were more expensive than I planned.
Ⓓ Hopefully, he'll sleep in the doghouse every night now.

PREWRITE Turn this paper over, and draw two lines dividing your paper into three sections. Label them *Morning, Midday,* and *Night*. In each section, list three things that a dog might do.

QUICKWRITE Describe a day in the life of a dog from the dog's point of view.

Writing Warm-up 65

1 Underline any adverbs in the sentence below.
His teacher gently tapped him on the shoulder to remind him to pay attention.

2 Edit the following sentence, and rewrite it on the line below.
her teacher was conserned that Liz wasnt understanding the math lesson

_____

3 Write three synonyms for the word *total* as in "a *total* mess."

_____ _____ _____

4 Revise the sentence below.
She asked us to rise our hands if we were ready to heard the next chapter.

_____

5 Which is the best sequence for these sentences?
¹**Our teacher told us she needed to talk to us after school.** ²**We said that we were laughing at a joke someone told us at recess.** ³**She asked us to show more respect next time.** ⁴**She asked us what we were doing during math class.**

Ⓐ 4-1-2-3   Ⓑ 3-1-4-2   Ⓒ 1-4-2-3   Ⓓ 2-4-3-1

6 Which sentence is most likely told from the teacher's point of view?
Ⓐ It's disruptive when I am giving instructions.
Ⓑ I didn't mean to laugh in class.
Ⓒ Next time I'll remember to show more respect to the rest of the class.
Ⓓ I just couldn't help myself.

PREWRITE Turn this paper over, and draw two lines dividing your paper into three sections. Label them *Morning, Midday,* and *Night.* In each section, list three things that a teacher might do.

QUICKWRITE Describe a day in the life of a teacher from the teacher's point of view.

Daily Writing Warm-ups 3–4 © 2006 Creative Teaching Press

Writing Warm-up 66

1 Underline any adverbs in the sentence below.
The salesman was eagerly trying to sell us a new car instead of a used car.

2 Edit the following sentence, and rewrite it on the line below.
mr martin ansered the add we had put in the paper to sell our car

_____

3 Write three synonyms for the word *old* as in "*old* car."

_____   _____   _____

4 Revise the sentence below.
After she washing her car, she went for a drived around the neighborhood.

_____

5 Which is the best sequence for these sentences?
**¹After the car accident, we needed a new car.
²After looking in the newspaper, we realized
that it was a smarter choice to buy a larger
used car. ³We drove to a few homes to see the
cars for sale. ⁴We settled on a two-year-old
car that had never had any problems.**

    Ⓐ 1-2-3-4   Ⓑ 1-4-2-3   Ⓒ 2-4-3-1   Ⓓ 3-1-4-2

6 Which sentence is most likely told from the car's point of view?
    Ⓐ I think a less expensive car will be better.
    Ⓑ Do you really think we will all fit inside?
    Ⓒ Well, it is my favorite color, and it's on sale.
    Ⓓ Why is my radio always on so loud?

PREWRITE Turn this paper over, and draw two lines dividing your paper into three sections. Label them *Morning, Midday,* and *Night.* In each section, list three things that a car might do.

QUICKWRITE Describe a day in the life of a car from the car's point of view.

Name_____ Date _____

Writing Warm-up 67

1 Underline any adverbs in the sentence below.
She was crying loudly all night long, because she was teething.

2 Edit the following sentence, and rewrite it on the line below.
her mother explaned that her brother was to young to no any better

_____

3 Write three synonyms for the word *bugs* as in "his crying *bugs* me."

_____   _____   _____

4 Revise the sentence below.
He has a bad habit of pulling my hair, and it really bugs me.

_____

5 Which is the best sequence for these sentences?
¹After school, I always did my homework first. ²Then, I would spend some time playing with my little brother. ³At other times, we would just play with his favorite stuffed animals. ⁴Sometimes we would watch cartoons or his baby videos together.

    Ⓐ 1-2-3-4   Ⓑ 1-2-4-3   Ⓒ 2-1-3-4   Ⓓ 3-2-1-4

6 Which sentence is most likely told from the point of view of a two-year-old?
    Ⓐ He keeps pulling my hair and crying, but I don't know what he wants.
    Ⓑ You need to understand that he's only a toddler, so he doesn't know how strong he is.
    Ⓒ I want that milk.
    Ⓓ Why don't you both go play together in the bedroom?

PREWRITE Turn this paper over, and draw two lines dividing your paper into three sections. Label them *Morning, Midday,* and *Night.* In each section, list three things that a two-year-old might do.

QUICKWRITE Describe a day in the life of a two-year-old from the toddler's point of view.

Writing Warm-up 68

1 Underline any adverbs in the sentence below.
The two scientists easily won the Nobel Prize for their discovery that cured a disease.

2 Edit the following sentence, and rewrite it on the line below.
the research fasility wanted to higher some scientists

_____

3 Write three synonyms for the word *sure* as in "he was *sure.*"

_____   _____   _____

4 Revise the sentence below.
The scientist was sure he made a new discovery.

_____

5 Which is the best sequence for these sentences?
¹After ten years, he finally came up with an idea. ²When he graduated, he decided that he wanted to focus on discovering ways to decrease pollution levels. ³In college, Mark had studied all areas of science. ⁴He hoped to figure out a way to help the environment by decreasing air and water pollution.

Ⓐ 1-4-3-2   Ⓑ 2-4-3-1   Ⓒ 2-1-3-4   Ⓓ 3-2-4-1

6 Which sentence is most likely told from the point of view of a scientist?
Ⓐ I don't know how he figured out the correct dose to give to that patient.
Ⓑ Where in the world will we ever find the money?
Ⓒ Science can include the study of the earth, animals, or people.
Ⓓ My first experiment was a failure, but I didn't give up.

PREWRITE Turn this paper over, and draw two lines dividing your paper into three sections. Label them *Morning, Midday,* and *Night*. In each section, list three things that a scientist might do.

QUICKWRITE Describe a day in the life of a scientist from the scientist's point of view.

Name_____   Date _____

Writing Warm-up 69

1 Underline any adverbs in the sentence below.
Although many people are terribly afraid of them, spiders are actually beneficial to humans in many ways.

2 Edit the following sentence, and rewrite it on the line below.
did you know their are many types of spider

_____

3 Write three synonyms for the word *scary*.

_____   _____   _____

4 Revise the sentence below.
Are you sures that you think spiders are scary?

_____

5 Which is the best sequence for these sentences?
¹I saw a spider dangling on what looked like a piece of string. ²After awhile, it got too dark to watch anymore, so I went to bed. ³The next morning, I saw two flies in the web. ⁴The spider began spinning a web.
Ⓐ 1-2-3-4   Ⓑ 1-4-2-3   Ⓒ 4-1-2-3   Ⓓ 2-3-1-4

6 Which sentence is most likely told from the point of view of a spider?
Ⓐ I won't hurt you if you won't hurt me.
Ⓑ Let me go get a shoe.
Ⓒ I'll knock it down with my broom.
Ⓓ I thought I sprayed for those spiders last week.

PREWRITE Turn this paper over, and draw two lines dividing your paper into three sections. Label them *Morning, Midday,* and *Night.* In each section, list three things that a spider might do.

QUICKWRITE Describe a day in the life of a spider from the spider's point of view.

Daily Writing Warm-ups 3–4 © 2006 Creative Teaching Press

Writing Warm-up 70

1 Underline any adverbs in the sentence below.
Her parents patiently waited in line to register her for the new school.

2 Edit the following sentence, and rewrite it on the line below.
do you agree that parents reprisent the hardest workers in the world

_____

3 Write three synonyms for the word *caring*.

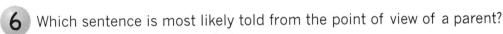

4 Revise the sentence below.
Parents always wanted the best for our kids.

_____

5 Which is the best sequence for these sentences?
¹**My sister Shari was crying and screaming in her room.** ²**Shari had blood coming out of her ear!** ³**My mom ran to see what was wrong.** ⁴**We rushed to the emergency room and found out she had a ruptured eardrum.**

    Ⓐ 1-4-3-2   Ⓑ 1-3-2-4   Ⓒ 4-1-3-2   Ⓓ 3-2-4-1

6 Which sentence is most likely told from the point of view of a parent?
    Ⓐ I didn't mean to do it.
    Ⓑ I don't want to.
    Ⓒ You just don't love me.
    Ⓓ I just want you to understand why that's important.

PREWRITE
Turn this paper over, and draw two lines dividing your paper into three sections. Label them *Morning, Midday,* and *Night.* In each section, list three things that a parent might do.

QUICKWRITE
Describe a day in the life of a parent from the parent's point of view.

Writing Warm-up 71

1 Underline any adverbs in the sentence below.
   The bird carefully built the nest for her future baby birds.

2 Edit the following sentence, and rewrite it on the line below.
   **birds work hard two arrang sticks feathers and leaves
   to build a next**

_____

3 Write three synonyms for the word *cute.*

_____   _____   _____

4 Revise the sentence below.
   It can be scary for a little bird when a cat comes up close.

_____

5 Which is the best sequence for these sentences?
   **¹In the spring, Lisa watched the baby birds hatch from the nests. ²She loved watching
   the birds take little pieces off her wreath to build their nests. ³It would be a holiday
   decoration that could go to good use in the spring. ⁴For the winter holiday, Lisa
   bought a wreath made out of feathers, fabric, and twigs.**

   Ⓐ 1-4-3-2   Ⓑ 2-4-3-1   Ⓒ 4-3-2-1   Ⓓ 3-2-4-1

6 Which sentence is most likely told from the point of view of a bird?
   Ⓐ If only I could find more soft feathers!
   Ⓑ I can't find my can opener.
   Ⓒ This looks like a warm tunnel.
   Ⓓ I'm too tired to do any more reading.

PREWRITE Turn this paper over, and draw two lines dividing your paper into three sections. Label them *Morning, Midday,* and *Night.* In each section, list three things that a bird might do.

QUICKWRITE Describe a day in the life of a bird from the bird's point of view.

Writing Warm-up 72

1 Underline any adverbs in the sentence below.
He cautiously helped the children cross the street.

2 Edit the following sentence, and rewrite it on the line below.
I dont know how the principal remembers all the familys names

_____

3 Write three synonyms for the word *easy* as in "an *easy* solution."

_____   _____   _____

4 Revise the sentence below.
The parent thought her daughter was too cute to ever get in trouble.

_____

5 Which is the best sequence for these sentences?
¹**Every Friday, the principal leads a flag ceremony for the entire school.** ²**It begins with the Pledge of Allegiance.** ³**We sing a song after the pledge.** ⁴**After the song, we listen to important announcements for the upcoming week.**

Ⓐ 1-4-3-2   Ⓑ 2-4-3-1   Ⓒ 4-3-2-1   Ⓓ 1-2-3-4

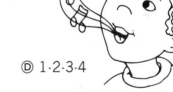

6 Which sentence is most likely told from the point of view of a principal?
Ⓐ You must follow the rules to keep other students safe.
Ⓑ You don't have to do your homework if you don't want to.
Ⓒ Please keep your desk neat at all times.
Ⓓ It's just too hard, so I think I'll take a nap.

PREWRITE Turn this paper over, and draw two lines dividing your paper into three sections. Label them *Morning, Midday,* and *Night*. In each section, list three things that a principal might do.

QUICKWRITE Describe a day in the life of a principal from the principal's point of view.

QUIZ 8

1 Underline any adverbs in the sentence below.

She lovingly hugged her mother to thank her for her unselfish help.

2 Edit the following sentence, and rewrite it on the line below.

wood you like to read a book solve a puzzle or watch a movie with me tonight

_____

3 Write three synonyms for the word *bugs* as in "it *bugs* me."

_____   _____   _____

4 Revise the sentence below.

I can't believed you think this old house is cute, because I think it's scary.

_____

5 Which is the best sequence for these sentences?

¹She was so tired, but she couldn't sleep. ²She decided that a nice, warm bath might help her relax. ³She knew that if she was relaxed, then she could sleep. ⁴After filling the bathtub with warm water and bubbles, she was ready for her relaxation time.

Ⓐ 1-3-2-4

Ⓑ 3-4-2-1

Ⓒ 4-1-3-2

Ⓓ 2-3-1-4

6 Which sentence is most likely told from the point of view of a pig?

Ⓐ I'm so misunderstood! I'm actually very clean!

Ⓑ What do you expect me to do for you?

Ⓒ Would you please come over and take me on a walk?

Ⓓ I want to cuddle with someone right now.

You can do it!

SCORE

Daily Writing Warm-ups 3–4 © 2006 Creative Teaching Press

Name_____ Date _____

Writing Warm-up 73

1 Underline any conjunctions in the sentence below.
She noticed that her mom had a rough day, so she made her a card to make her smile.

2 Edit the following sentence, and rewrite it on the line below.
shell have to by a gift by this wedesday so ill go to the store for her two save her time

_____

_____

3 Write one synonym and one antonym for the word *simple*.

_____   _____

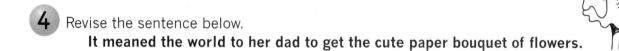

4 Revise the sentence below.
It meaned the world to her dad to get the cute paper bouquet of flowers.

_____

5 Which sentences would be the best to combine into one using a conjunction?
¹**I'll never forget the look on her face.** ²**I knew she was feeling sad.** ³**I decided to bake her a batch of her favorite chocolate chip cookies.** ⁴**Once they were baked, I wrapped them in wrapping paper on a plate.** ⁵**I told her to close her eyes.** ⁶**When she opened them, she was so surprised.** ⁷**The look on her face was priceless.**
Ⓐ 1-2   Ⓑ 2-3   Ⓒ 3-4   Ⓓ 4-5

6 "Doing kind things for others usually makes you feel good too." Which sentence is **not** relevant to the topic?
Ⓐ Awards have been given out to people for good deeds.
Ⓑ She felt happy and proud when she saw her friend's tears turn to a smile.
Ⓒ Giving her the bracelet made me feel good.
Ⓓ The card was made with love by her daughter.

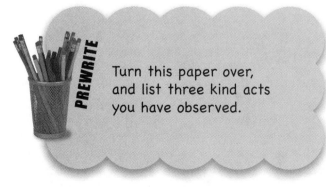
PREWRITE Turn this paper over, and list three kind acts you have observed.

QUICKWRITE Thinking of others . . . What is the kindest or most generous thing that you've observed someone doing?

Daily Writing Warm-ups 3–4 © 2006 Creative Teaching Press

91

Writing Warm-up 74

1 Underline any conjunctions in the sentence below.
Authors often dedicate their books to someone they love or are thankful to in some way.

2 Edit the following sentence, and rewrite it on the line below.
she hopped the publishing company wood like her book

_____

3 Write one synonym and one antonym for the word *finished*.

_____   _____

4 Revise the sentence below.
Since it was a good book, she decided to give copies to hers family members.

_____

5 Which sentences would be the best to combine into one using a conjunction?
¹**Authors spend many months writing their books.** ²**They can't do the fun activities they would normally do.** ³**Families sometimes suffer when authors must meet deadlines.** ⁴**The hard work and sacrifices they make often go unnoticed.** ⁵**That's often why there's a dedication page.** ⁶**It's a way of thanking those who suffered during the many months the book was being written.**

    Ⓐ 1-2   Ⓑ 2-3   Ⓒ 3-4   Ⓓ 4-5

6 "To dedicate a book to someone means to thank a person for his or her support while it was being written." Which sentence is **not** relevant to the topic?
    Ⓐ I remember that the author of my favorite book dedicated it to her boss and editor.
    Ⓑ Authors like having a page to say "thank you."
    Ⓒ A dedication page honors those people who believe in you.
    Ⓓ The person to whom a book is dedicated is recognized for his or her support.

PREWRITE Turn this paper over, and list three people who help you the most. Next to each name, write three ways he or she helps you.

QUICKWRITE Thinking of others . . . If you had one of your stories published, who would you mention on a dedication page? Why?

Daily Writing Warm-ups 3–4 © 2006 Creative Teaching Press

Writing Warm-up 75

1 Underline any conjunctions in the sentence below.
Sometimes a tree is planted to honor a baby's birth, because it represents new life.

2 Edit the following sentence, and rewrite it on the line below.
their are foundations that will plant a tree to honor a person

_____

3 Write one synonym and one antonym for the word *good* as in "a *good* idea."

_____   _____

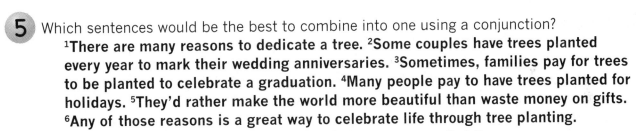

4 Revise the sentence below.
She planning to buyed a bouquet of flowers, but bought a potted plants instead.

5 Which sentences would be the best to combine into one using a conjunction?
[1]**There are many reasons to dedicate a tree.** [2]**Some couples have trees planted every year to mark their wedding anniversaries.** [3]**Sometimes, families pay for trees to be planted to celebrate a graduation.** [4]**Many people pay to have trees planted for holidays.** [5]**They'd rather make the world more beautiful than waste money on gifts.** [6]**Any of those reasons is a great way to celebrate life through tree planting.**

    Ⓐ 1-2   Ⓑ 2-3   Ⓒ 3-4   Ⓓ 4-5

6 "The companies that plant the trees to honor people also allow people to volunteer." Which sentence is **not** relevant to the topic?
    Ⓐ Volunteers plant the trees in national forests and urban cities.
    Ⓑ Volunteers prune and water the trees that have been planted
    Ⓒ Volunteers give informative talks and presentations to schools and clubs.
    Ⓓ To locate a tree-planting organization, simply search the Internet.

PREWRITE
Turn this paper over, and list three people who you think deserve to have a tree planted in their honor.

QUICKWRITE
Thinking of others . . .
If you could plant all three trees, who would you be honoring? Why? Where would you want them planted?

Writing Warm-up 76

1 Underline any conjunctions in the sentence below.

Homemade coupon books make great gifts, because you can create coupons specifically for the person receiving them.

2 Edit the following sentence, and rewrite it on the line below.

it maid such a difference to no that her father made the coupon book just for her

_____

3 Write one synonym and one antonym for the word *funny*.

_____   _____

4 Revise the sentence below.

They working together to maked ten good coupons for their dad.

_____

5 Which sentences would be the best to combine into one using a conjunction?

¹**The book gave three clever ideas for coupon books.** ²**The first one said, "I will rub your back for 15 minutes."** ³**Another one said, "I will make you breakfast in bed."** ⁴**The third idea was to give control of the television clicker for a whole week.** ⁵**That wasn't possible in our house.** ⁶**We don't even have a television!**

    Ⓐ 1-2   Ⓑ 2-3   Ⓒ 3-4   Ⓓ 4-5

6 "The students decided to make a secret coupon book for their teacher for Teacher Appreciation Week." Which sentence is **not** relevant to the topic?

    Ⓐ One coupon said, "We will all come in with sharpened pencils every day next week."
    Ⓑ They really liked their teacher.
    Ⓒ An idea was to add a coupon promising to never talk while she was talking.
    Ⓓ Bringing her hot cocoa every morning for a week was one child's idea.

PREWRITE Turn this paper over, and list three people who you would enjoy making a coupon book for as a surprise.

QUICKWRITE Thinking of others . . . If you made a coupon book for one person, who would it be? Why?

Daily Writing Warm-ups 3–4 © 2006 Creative Teaching Press

 *Writing Warm-up* **77**

1 Underline any conjunctions in the sentence below.
Getting packages in the mail is fun, because you never know what might be inside.

2 Edit the following sentence, and rewrite it on the line below.
the box was packed with little gifts includeing a bottle of perfume a red scarf

_____

3 Write one synonym and one antonym for the word *fast.*

_____   _____

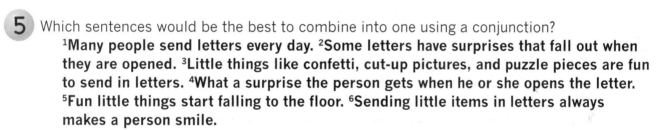

4 Revise the sentence below.
The letter was gonna arrive at her sister's house by Friday night.

_____

5 Which sentences would be the best to combine into one using a conjunction?
[1]Many people send letters every day. [2]Some letters have surprises that fall out when they are opened. [3]Little things like confetti, cut-up pictures, and puzzle pieces are fun to send in letters. [4]What a surprise the person gets when he or she opens the letter. [5]Fun little things start falling to the floor. [6]Sending little items in letters always makes a person smile.
    Ⓐ 1-2   Ⓑ 2-3   Ⓒ 3-4   Ⓓ 4-5

6 "The mail service will deliver almost any size letter or package to a home or business."
Which sentence is **not** relevant to the topic?
    Ⓐ Just remember that you need a stamp on the envelope.
    Ⓑ Postcards are often delivered from a person who is on vacation.
    Ⓒ Some people receive books and magazines through the mail.
    Ⓓ Many people have all of their holiday gifts delivered by the postal service.

PREWRITE Turn this paper over, and list three specific people who would enjoy getting something in the mail from you.

QUICKWRITE Thinking of others . . . If you had a few extra minutes to send something to someone in the mail, what would you send? To whom? Why?

Writing Warm-up 78

1 Underline any conjunctions in the sentence below.
   Giving someone a compliment shows you care, since you take the time to notice something about that person.

2 Edit the following sentence, and rewrite it on the line below.
   receiving a compliment is nice because it makes you feel good

_____

3 Write one synonym and one antonym for the word *old* as in "an *old* person."

_____   _____

4 Revise the sentence below.
   If you don't have anything nice to say, you shouldn't be saying anything at all.

_____

5 Which sentences would be the best to combine into one using a conjunction?
   ¹One creative teacher came up with a unique way of teaching her students how to give and receive sincere compliments. ²She bought little tin cans for each student. ³She bought blank business cards. ⁴Then she wrote a compliment for each student. ⁵The "compliment cards" were secretly placed in the students' compliment cans. ⁶Soon the students were writing compliment cards to one another!

   Ⓐ 1-2   Ⓑ 2-3   Ⓒ 3-4   Ⓓ 4-5

6 "A sincere compliment is one that you truly mean, not one that you say in order to get something you want." Which sentence is **not** relevant to the topic?
   Ⓐ If you say you like a boy's sweater just so he'll share his snack, then that's not a sincere compliment.
   Ⓑ Compliments always make someone feel good if you truly mean them.
   Ⓒ People should say anything that's on their minds.
   Ⓓ By giving a sincere compliment, you make others feel better.

PREWRITE
Turn this paper over, and list three specific compliments that would be sincere.

QUICKWRITE
Thinking of others . . .
If you wrote a compliment card for someone, who would it be for and what would it say? Why?

Daily Writing Warm-ups 3–4 © 2006 Creative Teaching Press

Name_____   Date _____

 *Writing Warm-up* 79

1 Underline any conjunctions in the sentence below.
Most children have many chores around the house, and they often receive an allowance for completing them.

2 Edit the following sentence, and rewrite it on the line below.
Niether brother liked to take out the trash, but someone had to do the chore

_____

3 Write one synonym and one antonym for the word *hard* as in "a *hard* chore."

_____   _____

4 Revise the sentence below.
Bill teached his little brother hows to brush his tooths.

_____

5 Which sentences would be the best to combine into one using a conjunction?
¹Chores teach children responsibility and teamwork. ²Every child should have to do chores. ³Although it may seem hard at first, children eventually appreciate the fact that they are helping the family. ⁴If you compare doing chores to sports teams, then children will understand the value even more. ⁵After all, every position on a team is important. ⁶By doing chores, children learn how to be responsible members of a team.

    Ⓐ 1-2   Ⓑ 2-3   Ⓒ 3-4   Ⓓ 4-5

6 "There are some chores that nearly every child dislikes." Which sentence is **not** relevant to the topic?
    Ⓐ Many children argue that they shouldn't have to do chores because they are only kids.
    Ⓑ Most children say they don't want to take out the trash.
    Ⓒ Another unpopular chore is washing the dirty dishes.
    Ⓓ The most common chore children dislike is cleaning their rooms.

PREWRITE Turn this paper over, and list three chores you don't like to do at home.

QUICKWRITE Thinking of others . . . If you would consider doing one chore for your family without being told, what would you do? Why?

Writing Warm-up 80

1 Underline any conjunctions in the sentence below.

Most parents will say that a homemade gift is the best, but sometimes children want to buy them an inexpensive gift.

2 Edit the following sentence, and rewrite it on the line below.

for valentines day i made my mom a card and picket sum fresh flowers for her

_____

3 Write one synonym and one antonym for the word *kind* as in "a *kind* gift."

_____   _____

4 Revise the sentence below.

Even though she had moneys to buyed a gift, she decided to make a gift by hand.

_____

5 Which sentences would be the best to combine into one using a conjunction?

¹Some children like to make gifts for special occasions. ²For example, they might make heart-shaped cards for birthdays. ³Some children choose to draw or paint pictures. ⁴They are homemade. ⁵The parents love them. ⁶Many parents even save the pictures in keepsake books for the child to see as an adult.

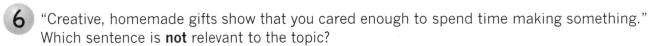

Ⓐ 1-2   Ⓑ 2-3   Ⓒ 3-4   Ⓓ 4-5

6 "Creative, homemade gifts show that you cared enough to spend time making something." Which sentence is **not** relevant to the topic?

Ⓐ Most parents love a little candy bar that includes a cute saying.

Ⓑ Homemade cards and pictures are always a huge hit with family members.

Ⓒ Stories written by you and stapled into a book show that you care.

Ⓓ Crafts made out of recycled materials show you took the time to create something.

PREWRITE
Turn this paper over, and list three things a family member would love to receive as a gift.

QUICKWRITE
Thinking of others . . . If you could buy or make anything at all for a family member, what would it be? Why?

Daily Writing Warm-ups 3–4 © 2006 Creative Teaching Press

Writing Warm-up 81

1 Underline any conjunctions in the sentence below.
She knew that her neighbor was sick in bed, so she made her a bowl of soup.

2 Edit the following sentence, and rewrite it on the line below.
if he didnt trim the tree, it could fall on his neighbors car in a storm

_____

3 Write one synonym and one antonym for the word *yummy* as in "a *yummy* dessert."

_____   _____

4 Revise the sentence below.
His neighbor breaked both of hers arms, so he helped her writed her letters.

_____

5 Which sentences would be the best to combine into one using a conjunction?
¹Keith's neighbors were always working, so he helped them when he could. ²One day, he put their trash cans away for them. ³He took their newspapers up to their front porch. ⁴There have been many times when he has walked lost dogs back to their houses in his neighborhood. ⁵He wants to treat his neighbors the way he hopes they would treat him.

Ⓐ 1-2   Ⓑ 2-3   Ⓒ 3-4   Ⓓ 4-5

6 "There are Web sites on the Internet that list many ideas for helping neighbors." Which sentence is **not** relevant to the topic?
Ⓐ The Internet is a valuable resource if you can't think of how to help your neighbors.
Ⓑ You simply search under "help others + list," and you'll have many choices.
Ⓒ Any search engine will help you locate lists of ways to help your neighbors.
Ⓓ You never know when you might need help yourself.

PREWRITE Turn this paper over, and list three things you could do for a neighbor.

QUICKWRITE Thinking of others . . . If you could do just one thing to help your next-door neighbor, what would it be? Why?

QUIZ 9

1 Underline any conjunctions in the sentence below.
Since she was starting her college classes soon, she needed to buy some books.

2 Edit the following sentence, and rewrite it on the line below.
she kneads to have a knew car by febuary so she can get to work

_____

3 Write one synonym and one antonym for the word *good as in* "a *good* book."

_____   _____

4 Revise the sentence below.
Mandy was gonna writed a cool message in a secret code.

_____

5 Which sentences would be the best to combine into one using a conjunction?
¹Every night after dinner, Lisa's golden retriever wanted dessert. ²She knew just what the dog was going to do. ³Right after dinner he would go get his ball. ⁴He would bring it to them. ⁵He waited until they threw the ball, and then he would chase after it. ⁶His reward was always a dog biscuit, since that was the only way he would drop the ball!

　　Ⓐ 1-2　　　　　Ⓑ 2-3　　　　　Ⓒ 3-4　　　　　Ⓓ 4-5

6 "Luckily, the gardeners were coming to do a few things over the weekend." Which sentence is **not** relevant to the topic?

　　Ⓐ The grass was dying, so they planned to dig it up and replace it with new grass.
　　Ⓑ Their neighbor asked them to trim the tree, because it could hit their roof in a storm.
　　Ⓒ The gardeners always arrived on time, so she wasn't worried.
　　Ⓓ The gardeners were going to move the palm tree from the backyard to the front yard to make more room for a barbecue.

Give your best effort!

SCORE

Daily Writing Warm-ups 3–4 © 2006 Creative Teaching Press

Writing Warm-up 82

1 Underline any prepositions in the sentence below.
The car drove quickly over the bridge to avoid getting stuck in the water.

2 Edit the following sentence, and rewrite it on the line below.
when driving a large vehicle, its always wize to be a caushous driver

_____

3 Circle the correct word.
You did a (well, good) job on your transportation report last week.

4 Revise the sentence below.
They couldn't getted on the bus, because they forgotted to bring money.

_____

5 Which sentence is the best example of using enriched vocabulary for the word "good"?
Ⓐ The bus driver on route 11 has a decent driving record.
Ⓑ What an excellent movie that was!
Ⓒ She thought it was an okay idea to ride bikes to the store.
Ⓓ He thought the white car would be just fine.

6 Which sentence has the most positive tone?
Ⓐ The car color didn't really matter to him, since he just wanted a safe vehicle.
Ⓑ She was thrilled to be buying her first bicycle.
Ⓒ The airplane was due to arrive early.
Ⓓ Modes of transportation are different around the world.

PREWRITE
Turn this paper over, and list five large things.

QUICKWRITE
So many similes . . . Choose a word from your list to complete the simile: "as big as a(n)_____." Use the phrase in a story.

Writing Warm-up 83

1 Underline any prepositions in the sentence below.
Beavers use their flat tails to steer while they swim in the water.

2 Edit the following sentence, and rewrite it on the line below.
when a beavers hungery youll find it eating leafs grasses and other water plants

_____

_____

3 Circle the correct word.
Beavers can build lodges very (good, well).

4 Revise the sentence below.
Beavers are strong swimmer, because they have webbed feet and thick, oily furs.

_____

5 Which sentence is the best example of using enriched vocabulary for the word "easy"?
   Ⓐ Beavers find it very simple to build lodges out of mud and branches.
   Ⓑ It's an effortless task for a beaver to chop down a tree with its teeth.
   Ⓒ A beaver finds it cinchy to stand up, since the tail helps hold up its body.
   Ⓓ It's not hard for a beaver to build a lodge for its family.

6 Which sentence has the most positive tone?
   Ⓐ Beavers can swim with branches in their mouths.
   Ⓑ Beavers do not hibernate in the winter.
   Ⓒ Wolves, coyotes, and bears are predators of beavers.
   Ⓓ Beavers are clever and strong, and they work as a team to build their lodges.

PREWRITE
Turn this paper over, and list five people that always seem to be busy.

QUICKWRITE
So many similes . . . Create a story using the simile: "as busy as a beaver" in your writing.

Name_____   Date _____

Writing Warm-up 84

1 Underline any prepositions in the sentence below.
There are many different species of owls that can be found around the world.

2 Edit the following sentence, and rewrite it on the line below.
although they are smart creatures, its a doubtfull that owls are as wise as they are shown in cartoons

_____

3 Circle the correct word.
Owls are (good, well) at flying silently through the night.

4 Revise the sentence below.
Owls rely most on their sense of hearing at night, because they also have good vision.

_____

5 Which sentence is the best example of using enriched vocabulary for the word "smart"?
   Ⓐ Owls are not foolish, because they have good memories.
   Ⓑ Owls are thought to be very, very smart.
   Ⓒ Do you consider owls to be intelligent birds?
   Ⓓ Most scientists agree that owls are very smart.

6 Which sentence has the most positive tone?
   Ⓐ Farmers welcome barn owls, since one barn owl can eat nearly 2,000 mice a year.
   Ⓑ Owls cannot really turn their heads all the way around.
   Ⓒ The snowy owl is found in the Arctic.
   Ⓓ Burrowing owls are an endangered species.

PREWRITE
Turn this paper over, and list five people that seem intelligent to you.

QUICKWRITE
So many similes . . . Make up a creative story using the simile "as wise as an owl" somewhere in your writing.

Writing Warm-up 85

1 Underline any prepositions in the sentence below.
   The natural habitat of the musk ox is the tundra.

2 Edit the following sentence, and rewrite it on the line below.
   she had to leave the oxen exhibit or shed be late to her doctor appointment

_____

3 Circle the correct word.
   Oxen protect their young very (good, well).

4 Revise the sentence below.
   The musk ox was nearby extinct until scientists were able to saved it.

_____

5 Which sentence is the best example of using enriched vocabulary for the word "big"?
   Ⓐ Teams of super-big oxen were once used to carry milk to the market.
   Ⓑ Oxen were so large and strong that they were used to pull carts on farms long ago.
   Ⓒ Due to the immense size and strength of oxen, they were often used to pull heavy loads.
   Ⓓ Some very big oxen could be used to do hard labor on a farm.

6 Which sentence has the most positive tone?
   Ⓐ In some countries, people still use oxen for farming.
   Ⓑ Oxen are male cows with long sharp horns.
   Ⓒ Oxen are much stronger and calmer than horses.
   Ⓓ When two oxen are used, they are usually hitched together with a wooden frame called a "yoke," which helps them work together.

PREWRITE
Turn this paper over, and list five people that seem strong to you.

QUICKWRITE
So many similes . . . Make up a creative story using the simile "as strong as an ox" somewhere in your writing.

Daily Writing Warm-ups 3–4 © 2006 Creative Teaching Press

Name_____   Date _____

Writing Warm-up 86

1 Underline any prepositions in the sentence below.
The Toulouse is a common goose found on a farm.

2 Edit the following sentence, and rewrite it on the line below.
he thought it was humorous when the goose chased his sister but he changed his mind win the goose started chasing him

_____

_____

3 Circle the correct word.
It was a (well, good) visit to the farm, because every student got to see baby geese.

4 Revise the sentence below.
Some Canada geese flies south for the winter, so some don't migrate at all.

_____

5 Which sentence is the best example of using enriched vocabulary for the words "a lot"?
Ⓐ There are a whole lot of geese throughout North America.
Ⓑ Geese eat a bunch of grass, grain, and berries.
Ⓒ Geese don't lay gobs of eggs.
Ⓓ Geese can be found on numerous farms in North America.

6 Which sentence has the most positive tone?
Ⓐ If geese are annoyed, they may chase after children.
Ⓑ Some people hunt geese.
Ⓒ A goose will often make children laugh when it waddles away quickly.
Ⓓ Every once in a while, a goose will be seen in a duck pond.

PREWRITE Turn this paper over, and list five characters on television or in books that seem silly to you.

QUICKWRITE So many similes . . . Make up a creative story using the simile "as silly as a goose" somewhere in your writing.

Writing Warm-up **87**

1 Underline any prepositions in the sentence below.
The dog jumped onto the couch to catch the ball.

2 Edit the following sentence, and rewrite it on the line below.
mandy was sick during her winter vacation so she couldnt ski sled or ice-skate

_____

3 Circle the correct answer.
He wasn't feeling (good, well), so his aunt took him to the doctor.

4 Revise the sentence below.
The doctor teached Joe which foods would created allergic reactions if eaten.

_____

5 Which sentence is the best example of using enriched vocabulary for the word *bad* as in "a *bad* cough"?

Ⓐ He had such a very bad cough that the doctor kept him out of school for a week.

Ⓑ He took medicine for his terrible cough.

Ⓒ His really bad cough was keeping him up at night.

Ⓓ He couldn't believe what an annoying cough he caught at school.

6 Which sentence has the most positive tone?

Ⓐ He would be feeling better soon.

Ⓑ Luckily, he was already on the road to recovery.

Ⓒ When a person is sick, they often loose energy.

Ⓓ It is important to drink lots of fluids when you are sick.

PREWRITE Turn this paper over, and list five times when you or a family member got sick.

QUICKWRITE So many similes . . . Make up a creative story using the simile "as sick as a dog" somewhere in your writing.

Writing Warm-up 88

1 Underline any prepositions in the sentence below.
The feathers she found on the hike fell out of her pocket.

2 Edit the following sentence, and rewrite it on the line below.
the sisters were planning a speshial surprise four there mom as a mothers day gift

_____

3 Circle the correct answer.
She thought the craft looked really (good, well).

4 Revise the sentence below.
At first, the picture in the craft magazine striked her as silly, so she soon discovered how cute it looked when finished.

_____

_____

5 Which sentence is the best example of using enriched vocabulary for the word *pretty* as in "a *pretty* feathered hat"?
    Ⓐ The attractive hat on the mannequin was made out of craft feathers.
    Ⓑ She made a really nice-looking napkin ring out of feathers.
    Ⓒ He wanted the cute, feathered wreath for his house.
    Ⓓ They thought the feathered boa was very pretty.

6 Which sentence has the most positive tone?
    Ⓐ Feathers can be used to make many different types of crafts and gifts.
    Ⓑ You should use craft feathers rather than real animal feathers when making projects.
    Ⓒ The down feathers gently protect the birds from the cold weather.
    Ⓓ Feathers float in the air, because they are so light.

PREWRITE
Turn this paper over, and list five things that can float in air.

QUICKWRITE
So many similes . . . Make up a creative story using the simile "as light as a feather" somewhere in your writing.

Writing Warm-up 89

1 Underline any prepositions in the sentence below.
One section of the marathon ran along the beach.

2 Edit the following sentence, and rewrite it on the line below.
the miniature bike trophy decorations were very creatif

_____

3 Circle the correct answer.
How (good, well) did you do on your history test last week?

4 Revise the sentence below.
They felt proud that them had spend the holiday fed the people who didn't have a home.

_____

5 Which sentence is the best example of using enriched vocabulary for the word *hard* as in "a *hard* race"?

Ⓐ She was amazed that she won the marathon, since it was such a challenging race.

Ⓑ He won the tough race with the fastest time.

Ⓒ They watched the really hard race hoping that their father would win.

Ⓓ Watching the fast race from their balcony was so much fun!

6 Which sentence has the most positive tone?

Ⓐ His report card showed that he had improved his grades.

Ⓑ They were so proud of their grades that they put their report cards on the refrigerator.

Ⓒ Their aunt paid them $10.00 for every "A" they received on their report card.

Ⓓ They wanted to do well in school to get into the college of their choice.

PREWRITE
Turn this paper over, and list five accomplishments.

QUICKWRITE
So many similes . . . Make up a creative story using the simile "as proud as a peacock" somewhere in your writing.

Daily Writing Warm-ups 3–4 © 2006 Creative Teaching Press

Writing Warm-up 90

1 Underline any prepositions in the sentence below.
The first person to finish the assignment is usually the one with the worst grade, because it takes time to do careful work in the classroom.

2 Edit the following sentence, and rewrite it on the line below.
the student were so excited because the day for their field trip had finaly arrived

_____

3 Circle the correct answer.
She did (good, well) on the project, because she took her time to do her best work.

4 Revise the sentence below.
They weared theys dressiest outfits to the birthday party.

_____

5 Which sentence is the best example of using enriched vocabulary for the word "easy"?
Ⓐ Shane thought it was so easy to solve the math problem.
Ⓑ Colby solved the simple math problem in less than a minute.
Ⓒ It took Dawn only a few seconds to answer the very easy math problem.
Ⓓ Victor took ten minutes to solve the short math problem.

6 Which sentence has the most positive tone?
Ⓐ Being the first to finish does not show that a person is smart, because smart people check their work.
Ⓑ If you are as smart as you look, then you will take your time to do neat and careful work.
Ⓒ I can tell that you took your time on this assignment, because you did quality work.
Ⓓ Many people believe that "slow and steady wins the race."

PREWRITE Turn this paper over, and list five times you or someone you know took the time to complete something well.

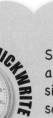

QUICKWRITE So many similes . . . Make up a creative story using the simile "as slow as a snail" somewhere in your writing.

QUIZ 10

1 Underline any prepositions in the sentence below.
The blimp flew across the sky during the football game.

2 Edit the following sentence, and rewrite it on the line below.
they were traveling to england france and germany with the choir

_____

3 Circle the best word choice in each sentence.

What a (good, well) job of painting the mural on the bedroom wall!

She wasn't feeling (good, well), so she decided to take a short nap.

He is such a (good, well) dog to sit at your feet before crossing the street.

How (good, well) do you think I did on this science fair project?

4 Revise the sentence below.
Sam wanted to drived instead of fly, although he was afraid of heights.

_____

5 Write an enriched vocabulary word for each of the following basic words.

smart _____   big _____

pretty _____   hard _____

6 Which sentence has the most positive tone?
Ⓐ They recycled their water bottles for money, because it helped their mother buy food.
Ⓑ By recycling water bottles, you help the environment and earn money at the same time.
Ⓒ Recycled water bottles can be exchanged for money or grocery store certificates.
Ⓓ They couldn't carry all of the recycled water bottles, because there were too many.

Show what you know!

SCORE

Daily Writing Warm-ups 3–4 © 2006 Creative Teaching Press

Writing Warm-up 91

1 Underline any nouns and circle any verbs in the following sentence.
If you learn to save money when you're young, then you will know how to save as an adult.

2 Edit the following sentence, and rewrite it on the line below.
she couldnt decide weather to exersise at the gym use the treadmill in her house

_____

3 Circle the correct answer.
She had a (bad, badly) habit of spending too much money.

4 Revise the sentence below.
Every year, the little town bank awarded a $50 savings bond to the kid who saved the more money.

_____

5 Write a topic sentence for the paragraph below.

_____

She already had $55.67. She hoped to earn another ten dollars every week in allowance. She was on her way to her goal of having $100. She wanted to be able to buy her mom a new coat for Mother's Day. With any luck, it would still be on sale by the time she had enough money. She wanted to show her mother how much she appreciated her hard work and sacrifices. It would be a terrific surprise!

6 Look at the paragraph in number 5. What is the biggest problem with the content?
Ⓐ varied sentence structure is needed
Ⓑ only a list of facts with no author's voice
Ⓒ 1–2 sentences do not belong with the others
Ⓓ none of the above

PREWRITE Turn this paper over, and list five reasons why saving money is smart.

QUICKWRITE Interpreter needed! . . . Read the following quote by Thomas Jefferson, and explain it in your own words. "Never spend your money before you have it."

Name_____   Date _____

Writing Warm-up 92

1 Underline any nouns and circle any adjectives in the following sentence.
Some people study dictionaries from a young age to learn about words.

2 Edit the following sentence, and rewrite it on the line below.
she was proud of her book sumery because she had worked hard

_____

3 Circle the correct answer.
Her head was hurting her so (bad, badly) that she had to rest in a quiet room.

4 Revise the sentence below.
If you wanna be a good doctor someday, then you should start preparing now.

_____

5 Write a topic sentence for the paragraph below.

_____

Ms. Johnson tries to create a safe and happy climate in her classroom. Children are responsible for following the same set of rules, and they must show respect to one another. Everyone helps out when there is a problem. Basically, her classroom functions as a team.

6 Look at the paragraph in number 5. What is the biggest problem with the content?
- Ⓐ varied sentence structure is needed
- Ⓑ only a list of facts with no author's voice
- Ⓒ 1–2 sentences do not belong with the others
- Ⓓ none of the above

PREWRITE Turn this paper over, and list five examples of times when it is important to be prepared.

QUICKWRITE Interpreter needed! . . . Read the following quote by Abraham Lincoln, and explain it in your own words. "I will prepare and someday my chance will come."

Writing Warm-up 93

1 Underline any verbs and circle any conjunctions in the following sentence.
If you ever see Joe lose his temper, then you will see the bad results that follow.

2 Edit the following sentence, and rewrite it on the line below.
jack was upset because he herd kids teasing him

_____

3 Circle the correct answer.
Yelling or raising your voice always results in making people feel (bad, badly).

4 Revise the sentence below.
The movie showed what happened when the main character got mad at his nice grandparents.

_____

5 Write a topic sentence for the paragraph below.

_____

By the time he got there, the first three awards would already be given. How would he ever win an award for his car if it wasn't there. He knew his car was better than the other cars. Joe wondered why there had to be so much traffic. He was so upset he could just scream! He was really worried that he wouldn't get there in time to enter his car into the contests.

6 Look at the paragraph in number 5. What is the biggest problem with the content?
   Ⓐ varied sentence structure is needed
   Ⓑ only a list of facts with no author's voice
   Ⓒ 1–2 sentences do not belong with the others
   Ⓓ none of the above

PREWRITE Turn this paper over, and list five examples of times when you or someone you knew was angry.

QUICKWRITE Interpreter needed! . . . Read the following quote by Confucius, and explain it in your own words. "When anger arises, think of the consequences."

Writing Warm-up 94

1 Underline any adjectives and circle any nouns in the following sentence.
Her favorite television show was about the man who made people's wishes come true.

2 Edit the following sentence, and rewrite it on the line below.
sarah was haveing a bad day but she new tomorrow wood be better

_____

3 Circle the correct answer.
I think that was a (bad, badly) decision in the first place.

4 Revise the sentence below.
The simple act of smiling at someone walked by can brighten that person's day.

_____

5 Write a topic sentence for the paragraph below.

_____

The lion was caught under a net. His paws were wrapped up in the net, so he couldn't claw his way out. Suddenly, a mouse walked by. The mouse began to gnaw on the net, and within moments the lion was free. The lion thanked the mouse for his act of kindness. After all, it saved his life! Simple things can make big differences in the lives of others.

6 Look at the paragraph in number 5. What is the biggest problem with the content?
Ⓐ varied sentence structure is needed
Ⓑ only a list of facts with no author's voice
Ⓒ 1–2 sentences do not belong with the others
Ⓓ none of the above

PREWRITE
Turn this paper over, and list five acts of kindness you have observed.

QUICKWRITE
Interpreter needed! . . . Read the following quote by Aesop, and explain it in your own words. "No act of kindness, no matter how small, is ever wasted."

Daily Writing Warm-ups 3–4 © 2006 Creative Teaching Press

Writing Warm-up 95

1 Underline any nouns and circle any verbs in the following sentence.
Just knowing facts does not help you succeed in life unless you know how to use those facts in creative ways.

2 Edit the following sentence, and rewrite it on the line below.
she didnt no how to begin her story because her ideas were hard to explain

_____

3 Circle the correct word.
I know I planned the party (bad, badly), but I think we can still have a good time.

4 Revise the sentence below.
Many successful inventors thinked of new ways to use stuff to make life easier.

_____

5 Write a topic sentence for the paragraph below.

_____

Every night before going to bed, Emily reads her invention journal. She adds new ideas or changes features of the ideas she already recorded. That reminds me of my friend who writes in his journal every night, too. Emily's plan is to become a famous inventor, so she records every idea in her journal. She knows that inventors use their imaginations to create new ideas. She can't wait to bring her ideas to life!

6 Look at the paragraph in number 5. What is the biggest problem with the content?

Ⓐ varied sentence structure is needed
Ⓑ only a list of facts with no author's voice
Ⓒ 1–2 sentences do not belong with the others
Ⓓ none of the above

PREWRITE
Turn this paper over, and list five reasons why it is important to have an imagination.

QUICKWRITE
Interpreter needed! . . . Read the following quote by Albert Einstein, and explain it in your own words. "Imagination is more important than knowledge."

Writing Warm-up 96

1 Underline any proper nouns and circle any conjunctions in the following sentence.

David is lucky, because his job is related to baseball, which is his favorite sport.

2 Edit the following sentence, and rewrite it on the line below.

its true that many jobs are difficult so you must be prepared to work hard

_____

3 Circle the correct answer.

Will there be (less, fewer) students in our classes this year?

4 Revise the sentence below.

She felt badder, because she had been drawing instead of working.

_____

5 Write a topic sentence for the paragraph below.

_____

As soon as young toddlers can move, they begin to play. That is how they learn to get along with others, share, and solve problems. Children should be encouraged to play outside with their friends as much as possible. As they get older, opportunities for play often go away. Many adults wish they could play. Play is an important part of growing up healthy and happy.

6 Look at the paragraph in number 5. What is the biggest problem with the content?
- Ⓐ varied sentence structure is needed
- Ⓑ only a list of facts with no author's voice
- Ⓒ 1–2 sentences do not belong with the others
- Ⓓ none of the above

PREWRITE
Turn this paper over, and draw a line down the middle. Label one side *Play* and the other *Work*. List five things you do for each.

QUICKWRITE
Interpreter needed! . . . Read the following quote by Theodore Roosevelt, and explain it in your own words. "When you play, play hard; when you work, don't play at all."

Daily Writing Warm-ups 3–4 © 2006 Creative Teaching Press

Writing Warm-up 97

1 Underline any verbs and circle any adverbs in the following sentence.
She was quietly hoping that her brother would learn his lesson and treat people kindly.

2 Edit the following sentence, and rewrite it on the line below.
the preparasion for the musical was going well until john tripped fell

_____

3 Circle the correct answer.
The speaker at the assembly was surprised to see (less, fewer) people than last year.

4 Revise the sentence below.
The baddest kid in class was always getted other people in trouble.

_____

5 Write a topic sentence for the paragraph below.

_____

Sue really wanted to be friends with Margo. She was willing to do anything. Sue let Margo take away her snacks at recess. She let Margo blame her when they got caught doing something wrong. Whatever Margo wanted, Sue was willing to do just so they would be friends. Is that what being a friend is all about?

6 Look at the paragraph in number 5. What is the biggest problem with the content?
    Ⓐ varied sentence structure is needed
    Ⓑ only a list of facts with no author's voice
    Ⓒ 1–2 sentences do not belong with the others
    Ⓓ none of the above

PREWRITE
Turn this paper over, and list five times when you felt someone let you down.

QUICKWRITE
Interpreter needed! . . . Read the following quote by Ralph Waldo Emerson, and explain it in your own words. "The only way to have a friend is to be one."

Name_____ Date _____

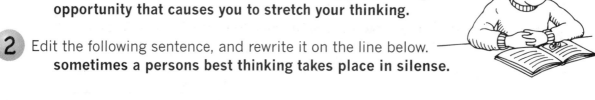

Writing Warm-up 98

1 Underline any adjectives and circle any verbs in the following sentence.

Always remember that a challenge is simply a learning opportunity that causes you to stretch your thinking.

2 Edit the following sentence, and rewrite it on the line below.

sometimes a persons best thinking takes place in silense.

_____

3 Circle the correct answer.

People who have (less, fewer) challenges end up with (less, fewer) new ideas or thoughts.

4 Revise the sentence below.

Successful people overcame many challenges before becomed who they is today.

_____

5 Write a topic sentence for the paragraph below.

_____

Rosa Parks was famous for refusing to give up her seat on a bus. She was also a key figure in starting the civil rights movement. She stood up for her own rights and made life better for future generations. Rosa Parks was an inspiration to many people. Thousands attended her funeral in 2005 to pay their respects. Rosa Parks faced challenges and paved the road to a better life for herself and others.

6 Look at the paragraph in number 5. What is the biggest problem with the content?
- Ⓐ varied sentence structure is needed
- Ⓑ only a list of facts with no author's voice
- Ⓒ 1–2 sentences do not belong with the others
- Ⓓ none of the above

PREWRITE Turn this paper over, and list five challenges you have faced.

QUICKWRITE Interpreter needed! . . . Read the following quote by Eleanor Roosevelt, and explain it in your own words. "You must do the thing you think you cannot do."

Daily Writing Warm-ups 3–4 © 2006 Creative Teaching Press

118

Writing Warm-up 99

1 Underline any nouns and circle any prepositions in the following sentence.
There are some countries of the world that try to create equality for every citizen.

2 Edit the following sentence, and rewrite it on the line below.
she needed to go back to skool but she didnt have enough money to by supplys

_____

3 Circle the correct answer.
People in poor countries have (less, fewer) clean water and sanitation.

4 Revise the sentence below.
An agreement between all three countries will help save the river.

_____

5 Write a topic sentence for the paragraph below.

_____

Saving habitats that are being destroyed will result in fewer endangered species. The development of solar vehicles will lessen our need for gas and help decrease air pollution. The search for vaccines to prevent diseases is also a much needed effort. These are just a few of the many ways people around the world are trying to help each other.

6 Look at the paragraph in number 5. What is the biggest problem with the content?
Ⓐ varied sentence structure is needed
Ⓑ only a list of facts with no author's voice
Ⓒ 1-2 sentences do not belong with the others
Ⓓ none of the above

PREWRITE Turn this paper over, and list five unfair situations you have observed.

QUICKWRITE Interpreter needed! . . . Read the following quote by Martin Luther King Jr., and explain it in your own words. "Injustice anywhere is a threat to justice everywhere."

Name_____   Date _____

QUIZ 11

1 Label the part of speech for each word that is listed below the sentence.

They cautiously entered the cave, because they didn't know whether or not a bear was using it as a den.

they _____   cautiously _____

entered _____   cave _____

because _____   as _____

2 Edit the following sentence, and rewrite it on the line below.

mandy didnt no what to get her mom for her birthday so she made her a card

_____

3 Circle the correct answer in each sentence.

There are (less, fewer) ants in the backyard this year.

Would you like to have (less, fewer) homework on weekends?

She knew she did a (bad, badly) job of explaining her point of view.

She was hurt (bad, badly) in the fall.

4 Revise the sentence below.

If you have unused stuff in your home you can donating them to a charity.

_____

5 Write a topic sentence for the paragraph below.

_____

It will be held on Friday and Saturday. Six teachers are going to the conference. They are looking forward to learning new ideas about math. The conference takes place every year.

6 Look at the paragraph in number 5. What is the biggest problem with the content?

  Ⓐ varied sentence structure is needed
  Ⓑ only a list of facts with no author's voice
  Ⓒ 1–2 sentences do not belong with the others
  Ⓓ none of the above

SCORE

Daily Writing Warm-ups 3–4 © 2006 Creative Teaching Press

ANSWER KEY

For items 4, 5, and 6 accept any reasonable response that students are able to defend.

Writing Warm-up 1

1. bed, teeth
2. **Did** you remember to hang your towel on the bar**?**
3. D
4. She packed a large lunch, but she didn't eat one **bite** at school.
5. B
6. D

Writing Warm-up 2

1. character, book
2. **I** remember the title, but what was that story **about?**
3. D
4. My little sister is not **(friendly, kind)** to me, because sometimes she **bites** me to get her way.
5. D
6. A

Writing Warm-up 3

1. house, family
2. **Can** you name **every** member of your family**?**
3. A
4. All of the members in Dave's loving family **grew** up sharing one small apartment.
5. A
6. C

Writing Warm-up 4

1. talent, ability
2. **I know** how to do a cartwheel and a back flip**.**
3. C
4. Practicing every day was **(challenging, difficult)**, but it helped Jill's knowledge of swimming techniques **to grow** over time.
5. C
6. D

Writing Warm-up 5

1. pet peeve
2. **Did** you see how often he chewed with his mouth open at **tonight's** dinner**?**
3. C
4. His pet peeve is when his daughter says, "That's all I get?" when he **buys** her something.
5. B
6. D

Writing Warm-up 6

1. subjects, school, reading, writing, math
2. **In school**, math seems to be my best subject every year**.**
3. B
4. I think I'm **(smart, intelligent, clever)** when it comes to solving math problems because I **solve** them in my head.
5. C
6. C

Writing Warm-up 7

1. weekends, children, cartoons, morning, outside, friends
2. **It's almost** time for you to go to bed now**.**
3. C
4. We have **(exciting, enjoyable)** activities planned for the weekend, including **building** my new bed and **painting** the walls.
5. D
6. D

Writing Warm-up 8

1. dad, story, night, bed
2. **She** wanted to stay up an hour later **because** her favorite show was delayed**.**
3. A
4. After she tucked her son in bed, she began **building** a triple-layer cake for his party.
5. B
6. C

Writing Warm-up 9

1. students, homework
2. **Did** you **know** that doing your homework is one way to become an even better student**?**
3. A
4. His goal was to improve his grades, so he **hit** the books and tried studying harder.
5. C
6. A

QUIZ 1

1. dog, cats, rabbits, house
2. **I'm** going to the doctor **again, because I** can't get rid of my sore throat**.**
3. A
4. When the number of children in her family **hit** five, Mrs. Brown realized she had **outgrown** her house.

5. Possible answer: Jenny was eager for her vacation to begin.
6. D

Writing Warm-up 10

1. is, elected
2. **Have** you heard about the **Air Force One** exhibit at the presidential library**?**
3. C
4. They are trying to **build** a new set of laws to help the president boost the economy.
5. A
6. D

Writing Warm-up 11

1. is, have, pay, cook, work
2. **I** need to take a **snack** to the movies or **I'll** be starving**!**
3. D
4. Do you like the tree house my dad and I **built?**
5. A
6. A

Writing Warm-up 12

1. want, become, must, earn
2. **Do** you have **enough** experience flying planes to earn a license**?**
3. D
4. The need for **(trained, excellent)** pilots is still **growing** in some private airline companies.
5. C
6. D

Writing Warm-up 13

1. require
2. **Do** you find it **difficult** to fall asleep at bedtime**?**
3. A
4. Do you think you need more sleep as you **grow** older?
5. C
6. A

Writing Warm-up 14

1. live, get, meet
2. **Did** you know that a **driver's license** allows you to drive in any state**?**
3. D
4. The home team was **hitting** the ball so hard that the visiting team had no chance of winning.
5. A
6. D

Writing Warm-up 15

1. included
2. **Would** you **believe** me if **I** told you that **they're** taking chicken nuggets off the menu**?**
3. D
4. All of the students cheered when they saw the **(delicious, tasty)** cupcakes on the menu.
5. A
6. C

Writing Warm-up 16

1. is, protect
2. **He finally** received the letter saying he was accepted into the **United States Air Force.**
3. A
4. Do you think he's **grown** up enough for such a **(large, enormous, important)** responsibility?
5. A
6. A

Writing Warm-up 17

1. wanted, sail
2. **She always** asks her mother for **advice** before **making** important decisions.
3. B
4. The captain **bought** rafts and life jackets for the **(large, massive, enormous)** ship.
5. D
6. C

Writing Warm-up 18

1. called, said
2. **He usually didn't** say bad words, but when he did, **he** was disciplined**.**
3. C
4. The boy **hit** the girl after she **took** the ball from him.
5. B
6. D

QUIZ 2

1. had, make, wash, sweep
2. **Did** she **have** a **difficult** time deciding which vacuum to buy at the store**?**
3. B
4. She got a **(terrific, fantastic, great)** award at home, because she **hit** the ball the farthest in the game.
5. Possible answer: Lisa wanted to lose weight.
6. D

Writing Warm-up 19

1. nouns: cookies, soda

---

verbs: loved, eat, drink
2. **It's** not a good idea to eat cookies, candy, pretzels, and chocolate before dinner**.**
3. A
4. They wanted to eat the **(delicious, tasty)** cookies, but they **knew** their baby brother would tell.
5. A
6. D

Writing Warm-up 20

1. nouns: spaghetti, table
   verbs: slurped, burped
2. **She couldn't believe** that the girl just burped for the **fourth** time!
3. A
4. Those children sure **(need, needed)** lessons on good manners.
5. A
6. A

Writing Warm-up 21

1. nouns: people, cookies, milk
   verbs: dip, get
2. **He easily** twisted the top off the cookie and then licked the frosting**.**
3. B
4. They **took** the cookies out of the package and **ate** them all before dinner.
5. D
6. A

Writing Warm-up 22

1. nouns: french fries, hamburgers
   verb: eats
2. **Do** you **know** that she **usually** eats there at least once a week**?**
3. A
4. The neighbors **told** the city that they needed some **(delicious, tasty)** fast-food restaurants in their town.
5. B
6. B

Writing Warm-up 23

1. nouns: summer, people, sundaes
   verb: eat
2. **Would** you eat ice cream even **though** you were allergic to dairy products**?**
3. A
4. The kids **thought** of **(creative, fun, tasty, delicious)** toppings for their **(frozen, frosty, chilly)** sundaes.
5. B
6. A

Writing Warm-up 24

1. nouns: jalapenos, peppers, dishes

---

verbs: are, used
2. **Is** it true that the chef is **trying** to **develop** a new recipe using jalapeno peppers**?**
3. B
4. Chef Norton ~~was~~ thought she had a new twist for making **(tasty, delicious)** breadsticks.
5. A
6. C

Writing Warm-up 25

1. nouns: Carina, food, brother, food
   verbs: loves, eat, likes
2. **Getting** the right **quantity** of noodles, onions, and zucchini in the stir-fry mix is important**.**
3. B
4. She liked many different foods as long as they tasted **(delicious, yummy)**.
5. B
6. D

Writing Warm-up 26

1. nouns: cruise, dessert, dinner
   verbs: ordered, would, be, enjoy
2. **When** eating a meal, should you begin with the salad, the main course, or the dessert**?**
3. B
4. She asked the waiter, "Would you please **show** me the dessert tray?"
5. A
6. C

Writing Warm-up 27

1. noun: salad   verbs: think, tastes
2. **If you're through** with your plates, then **I'll** go wash the dishes, put them away, and bring out dessert**.**
3. D
4. He **told** the waiter he would like to order soup.
5. D
6. D

QUIZ 3

1. nouns: earthquake, Lynn's, rabbit, dog
   verbs: thumped, barked
2. **Would** you rather picnic in the park, swim in a pool, or collect shells at the beach**?**
3. B
4. Did you hear that she **told** the teacher that her friends were **talking** behind her back?
5. Possible answer: Doing chores helps a family work together.
6. D

Writing Warm-up 28

1. she
2. **Would** you mind helping me by **taking** this shirt to the cleaners after work?
3. A
4. Her (**strange, unusual**) pair of pants got the attention of all the (**students, children**) in **her** class.
5. A
6. D

Writing Warm-up 29

1. They, their
2. **Does** the postal worker standing over **there** look **familiar?**
3. B
4. She rarely had any free time, since her (**demanding, difficult, challenging**) job kept her very busy all day.
5. C
6. C

Writing Warm-up 30

1. it
2. **How often** do you watch television instead of play outside?
3. B
4. He **took** his time doing his homework so his dad wouldn't **say** he didn't use **his** time well.
5. A
6. C

Writing Warm-up 31

1. Her, she, her
2. **People often develop** bad habits without even **realizing it.**
3. A
4. What a (**ridiculous, foolish, silly**) idea to let the clothes pile up for a month before **washing them.**
5. A
6. A

Writing Warm-up 32

1. you, his
2. **She** was **beginning** to **think** that she might want to try out for soccer after all.
3. D
4. She **thought** basketball was (**an exciting, a thrilling**) sport, but she wasn't sure she would be (**have the talent for, have the ability for**) at it.
5. A
6. C

Writing Warm-up 33

1. them

2. **He** told her that his **favorite** beverages are lemonade, milk, and juice.
3. C
4. Do you agree with **me** think that he shouldn't drink soda until he's a teenager?
5. A
6. A

Writing Warm-up 34

1. they, themselves
2. **Would** you **choose** to live on **an** island, in the **desert**, or on a ranch?
3. A
4. Do you think a tent is a **comfortable** place to live, or do you think a tent is (**a horrible, a terrible, an uncomfortable**) home?
5. C
6. D

Writing Warm-up 35

1. she
2. **She** thinks **she'll probably** get a pet ferret when she **grows** up.
3. A
4. Don't you think that a rabbit **makes** a (**wonderful, fabulous, marvelous**) pet for showing a child how to be kind?
5. C
6. D

Writing Warm-up 36

1. She, her, her
2. **You would** be **lonely** if you **lost** your friends because you **didn't** play nicely.
3. B
4. He **knew** he made a (**poor**) choice when he **said** that his dog ate his homework.
5. A
6. D

QUIZ 4

1. you, her, she, us
2. **She** was shocked when she heard that the **amount** of cookies she made was **probably** not **enough** for the **whole** class.
3. A
4. She **told** the teacher that **she slid** down the slide backwards.
5. Possible answer: Making lotion is more complex than you might think.
6. A

Writing Warm-up 37

1. nouns: book, part   pronouns: He, he
2. **The Book Lovers' Club** required each member to record the **number** of pages read nightly.

3. B
4. He **forgot** to return his library book on time, so he was charged a (**small, tiny**) fine of 25 cents.
5. D
6. C

Writing Warm-up 38

1. nouns: school, plan, years
   pronoun: its
2. **My calendar** shows that this weekend is the **Founder's Day** celebration at **Lee School.**
3. B
4. You can't **go** to the school play, because **your** homework isn't done.
5. B
6. D

Writing Warm-up 39

1. nouns: goal, baskets, game
   pronouns: He, his
2. **Do** you have the information **about** the parent conferences?
3. C
4. I **forgot** to write down **my** goals for the week, but I remember most of **them.**
5. D
6. A

Writing Warm-up 40

1. nouns: uniforms, morning
   pronoun: they
2. **Why** does **everybody** wear those untucked shirts, giant belts, and baggy jeans?
3. B
4. He looked so (**ridiculous, foolish**) wearing black pants that were ten sizes too big!
5. A
6. A

Writing Warm-up 41

1. nouns: opinion, computer, invention, time
   pronoun: my
2. **Would** it be **impossible** to live in modern times without computers?
3. C
4. She was trying to think of (**an interesting, an exciting, a creative**) invention that could help her **finish** her chores.
5. D
6. C

Writing Warm-up 42

1. nouns: train, zoo, weekend
   pronouns: you, us
2. **I think it's** the **prettiest** garden that

I've ever seen in a city.
3. A
4. Why did she dream that she couldn't live without her watch?
5. A
6. B

Writing Warm-up 43

1. noun: kits   pronouns: you, we, our
2. She couldn't find the flashlights, candles, or radio in all the confusion.
3. A
4. She felt safe with her family even though the house was dark and scary.
5. A
6. D

Writing Warm-up 44

1. nouns: Hannah, name
   pronouns: her, it
2. Can you think of somebody who has a name you simply love?
3. B
4. He dreamt that he had forgotten his name on the first day of school!
5. C
6. A

Writing Warm-up 45

1. nouns: author, bookstore, weekend
   pronouns: you, your
2. Did you meet that famous football player when he came to our school?
3. A
4. She forgot that she shouldn't shine the light right into the actor's face.
5. B
6. A

Quiz 5

1. nouns: idea, folder, comic strips
   pronouns: you, he, our
2. It was hard for everybody to agree on a new design for the school calendar.
3. C
4. She felt so tired after helping her sister that she sat down to rest.
5. D
6. A

Writing Warm-up 46

1. sad, realistic
2. Would you buy popcorn, candy, and a hot dog at the movies?
3. C
4. She thought the movie was so (amusing, humorous, hysterical) that she almost choked on her popcorn.
5. A
6. B

Writing Warm-up 47

1. healthy
2. She decided to buy a calendar to list the sweet, salty, and crunchy snacks she ate each day.
3. B
4. He packed some (smart, healthy) snacks to eat at recess.
5. B
6. C

Writing Warm-up 48

1. fluffy, yellow, animal
2. There were several cats, dogs, and rabbits at the animal shelter.
3. B
4. They had forgotten that the (adorable) kitten couldn't be adopted until it was eight weeks old.
5. D
6. D

Writing Warm-up 49

1. sports, fast, more
2. She went to the doctor, dentist, and car dealership with her family.
3. A
4. He forgot to make an appointment to test drive the (speedy), new sports car.
5. D
6. C

Writing Warm-up 50

1. intelligent, responsible, many
2. Mr. Jones had such an incredible class that he smiled all the time.
3. A
4. What do you think it takes to be (an excellent, a fantastic, a terrific) student every year in school?
5. D
6. B

Writing Warm-up 51

1. large, roomy, crowded
2. The large home in Yountville was a real bargain compared to the small, expensive home in the city.
3. A
4. Her room was so (large, spacious, enormous, extensive) that it could fit a king-size bed and two dressers!
5. C
6. A

Writing Warm-up 52

1. young, sparkly, night
2. She loves to count the stars, look for planets, and watch the moon at night.

3. C
4. On Tori's way out of the door, her mother said, "Have a nice day."
5. B
6. C

Writing Warm-up 53

1. hot, cold
2. They had already waited over an hour for the pizza delivery to arrive.
3. C
4. Her (amusing, humorous) friends called her "Pizza Queen," since she always made the best pizza!
5. B
6. D

Writing Warm-up 54

1. Last, beautiful, spacious
2. Do you notice the scent of freshly cooked salmon coming from that restaurant?
3. D
4. On a typical summer day, you will find the boys swimming in their backyard pool.
5. B
6. B

QUIZ 6

1. tiny, colorful, backyard
2. The site of Dr. Ann's new office had been chosen.
3. D
4. She forgot to do her homework, so she dreamt she had to stay after school.
5. D
6. A

Writing Warm-up 55

1. nouns: party, rink, weekend
   adjectives: birthday, skating
2. Who would you name as your closest, kindest, and most thoughtful friend?
3. Possible answers include: kind, helpful, loving, thoughtful
4. Do you think you are a (kind, helpful, loving) friend to others?
5. A
6. D

Writing Warm-up 56

1. nouns: child, parents
   adjectives: respectful, loving
2. Why is that big, green grasshopper on your ceiling?
3. Possible answers include: inform, instruct, advise, educate
4. It's a fact of life that you don't always get to do what you want to do.

5. C
6. C

Writing Warm-up 57

1. nouns: island, Hawaii, December
   adjectives: beautiful, tropical
2. **Are** you visiting the museum, tropical gardens, and ancient ruins while in **Mexico?**
3. Possible answers include: eventful, exciting, fun, thrilling
4. Did I **tell** you what a (**terrific, fantastic, wonderful**) vacation I had last year in Africa?
5. D
6. C

Writing Warm-up 58

1. nouns: vitamins, morning, Katie, girl
   adjectives: chewable, every, strong, healthy
2. **Do** you **know** that **everybody** needs to take better care of **their** teeth, skin, and bones**?**
3. Possible answers include: intelligent, wise, well-informed, thoughtful
4. He **rose** when the presenter said, "Please stand up if **you drink** at least one glass of milk every day."
5. A
6. A

Writing Warm-up 59

1. nouns: people, chores, others, money
   adjectives: some, unpleasant, extra
2. **Julie stopped** shopping on the Internet when she realized she was spending **too** much money**.**
3. Possible answers include: foolish, unwise, wasteful, ridiculous
4. It's a (**smart, wise, intelligent**) (**decision, idea**) that she didn't waste her money on the video game player, because a **better** one is coming out soon.
5. A
6. B

Writing Warm-up 60

1. nouns: sandwich, lettuce, tomato
   adjectives: submarine, fresh
2. **Police** officer **Williams** was the first person on the **scene** after the alarm sounded**.**
3. Possible answers include: delicious, scrumptious, tasty
4. The sandwich he **ordered** tasted so (**terrible, disgusting**) that he **took** it right back to the shop.
5. B

6. C

Writing Warm-up 61

1. nouns: skills, job
   adjectives: math, necessary, every
2. **It's amazing** how you solved that problem without using your fingers, a calculator, or a pencil and paper**.**
3. Possible answers include: difficult, challenging, tough
4. She was such a (**clever, intelligent, wise**) student that she could solve (**difficult, challenging**) math problems in **her** head.
5. B
6. A

Writing Warm-up 62

1. nouns: photographers, years, photos, images
   adjectives: professional, clear, colorful
2. **Did** you **see** the article in **Wednesday's** paper describing the upcoming photo contest**?**
3. Possible answers include: a few, a couple of, a small number of
4. She **fell** off the log trying to **take** pictures of the baby bird **sleeping** in the nest.
5. B
6. A

Writing Warm-up 63

1. nouns: job, time, money, chimpanzees, Africa
   adjectives: her, her, wild
2. **Is** the auction going to be on **Tuesday** or **Wednesday** of next **week?**
3. Possible answers include: a great deal, numerous amounts, a great sum
4. John **read** the brochure while he **waited** for the program to begin.
5. C
6. A

QUIZ 7

1. nouns: hot chocolate, cream, sprinkles
   adjectives: raspberry, whipped, chocolate
2. **Didn't** you think the first **scene** of the play was **amazing?**
3. Possible answers include: clever, useful, excellent, creative
4. The (**tasty, delicious, scrumptious**) ice-cream sandwich was melting all **over** her clothes.
5. A
6. B

Writing Warm-up 64

1. quietly
2. **Did** he like the squeaky bone, the stuffed animal, or tennis ball the best**?**
3. Possible answers include: thought, belief, guess
4. That silly dog **thought** it was so (**exciting, thrilling, enjoyable**) to **run** around the house with a shoe in its mouth.
5. A
6. B

Writing Warm-up 65

1. gently
2. **Her** teacher was **concerned** that Liz **wasn't** understanding the math lesson.
3. Possible answers include: complete, entire, utter
4. She asked us to **raise** our hands if we were ready to **hear** the next chapter.
5. C
6. A

Writing Warm-up 66

1. eagerly
2. **Mr. Martin answered** the **ad** we had put in the paper to sell our car.
3. Possible answers include: ancient, aged, antique
4. After she **washed** her car, she went for a **drive** around the neighborhood.
5. A
6. D

Writing Warm-up 67

1. loudly
2. **Her** mother **explained** that her brother was **too** young to **know** any better.
3. Possible answers include: annoys, irritates, disturbs, bothers
4. He has a (**terrible**) habit of pulling my hair, and it really (**annoys, bothers, irritates**) me.
5. B
6. C

Writing Warm-up 68

1. easily
2. **The** research **facility** wanted to **hire** some scientists**.**
3. Possible answers include: positive, certain, clear, confident
4. The scientist was (**certain, confident**) he made a new discovery.
5. D
6. D

Writing Warm-up 69

1. terribly, actually
2. **Did** you know **there** are many types of **spiders?**
3. Possible answers include: frightening, creepy, spooky, terrifying
4. Are you **sure** that you think spiders are **(frightening, creepy, spooky, terrifying)?**
5. B
6. A

Writing Warm-up 70

1. patiently
2. **Do** you agree that parents **represent** the hardest workers in the world?
3. Possible answers include: loving, nurturing, friendly, warm-hearted
4. Parents always **want** the best for **their children.**
5. B
6. D

Writing Warm-up 71

1. carefully
2. **Birds** work hard **to arrange** sticks, feathers, and leaves to build a **nest.**
3. Possible answers include: adorable, precious, sweet
4. It can be **(frightening, terrifying)** for a little bird when a cat comes up close.
5. C
6. A

Writing Warm-up 72

1. cautiously
2. I **don't** know how the principal remembers all the **families'** names.
3. Possible answers include: simple, basic, effortless, painless
4. The parent **thought** her daughter was too **(adorable, sweet, precious)** to ever get in trouble.
5. D
6. A

QUIZ 8

1. lovingly
2. **Would** you like to read a book, solve a puzzle, or watch a movie with me tonight?
3. Possible answers include: bothers, annoys, irritates, disturbs
4. I can't **believe** you think this **(old, ancient)** house is **(adorable, charming),** because I think it's **(frightening, terrible).**
5. A
6. A

Writing Warm-up 73

1. so
2. **She'll** have to **buy** a gift by this **Wednesday,** so **I'll** go to the store for her **to** save her time.
3. synonyms: easy, basic
   antonyms: hard, difficult, challenging
4. It **meant** the world to her dad to get the **(adorable, precious, darling)** paper bouquet of flowers.
5. B
6. A

Writing Warm-up 74

1. or
2. **She hoped** the publishing company **would** like her book.
3. synonyms: done, completed
   antonyms: ongoing, unfinished, continuing
4. Since it was **(an excellent, a terrific)** book, she decided to give copies to **her** family members.
5. B
6. A

Writing Warm-up 75

1. because
2. **There** are foundations that will plant a tree to honor a person.
3. synonyms: smart, wise
   antonyms: foolish, unwise
4. She **planned** to **buy** a bouquet of flowers, but bought a potted **plant** instead.
5. D
6. D

Writing Warm-up 76

1. because
2. **It made** such a difference to **know** that her father made the coupon book just for her.
3. synonyms: humorous, amusing
   antonyms: sad, serious, depressing
4. They **worked** together to **make** ten **(fantastic, unique, exciting)** coupons for their dad.
5. D
6. B

Writing Warm-up 77

1. because
2. **The** box was packed with little gifts, **including** a bottle of perfume **and** a red scarf.
3. synonyms: quick, speedy
   antonym: slow
4. The letter was **going to** arrive at her sister's house by Friday night.

5. D
6. A

Writing Warm-up 78

1. since
2. **Receiving** a compliment is nice, because it makes you feel good.
3. synonyms: aged, elderly
   antonyms: young, youthful
4. If you don't have anything **(kind, loving, thoughtful)** to say, you shouldn't ~~be~~ **say** anything at all.
5. B
6. C

Writing Warm-up 79

1. and
2. **Neither** brother liked to take out the trash, but someone had to do the chore.
3. synonyms: difficult, tiring
   antonyms: simple, easy
4. Bill **taught** his little brother **how** to brush his **teeth.**
5. A
6. A

Writing Warm-up 80

1. but
2. **For Valentine's Day, I** made my mom a card and **picked some** fresh flowers for her.
3. synonyms: thoughtful, caring
   antonyms: mean, heartless, cruel
4. Even though she had **money** to **buy** a gift, she decided to make a gift by hand.
5. D
6. A

Writing Warm-up 81

1. so
2. **If** he **didn't** trim the tree, it could fall on his **neighbor's** car in a storm.
3. synonyms: delicious, tasty
   antonyms: disgusting, terrible
4. His neighbor **broke** both of **her** arms, so he helped her **write** her letters.
5. B
6. D

QUIZ 9

1. Since
2. **She needs** to have a **new** car by **February,** so she can get to work.
3. synonyms: excellent, wonderful, fantastic
   antonyms: terrible, horrible
4. Mandy was **going to write (a fabulous, a terrific, an amazing)** message in a

secret code.
5. C
6. C

Writing Warm-up 82

1. over, to, in
2. **When** driving a large vehicle, **it's** always **wise** to be a **cautious** driver.
3. good
4. They couldn't **get** on the bus, because they **forgot** to bring money.
5. B
6. B

Writing Warm-up 83

1. to, in
2. **When** a **beaver is hungry, you'll** find it eating **leaves,** grasses, and other water plants**.**
3. well
4. Beavers are strong **swimmers,** because they have webbed feet and thick, oily **fur**.
5. B
6. D

Writing Warm-up 84

1. of, around
2. **Although** they are smart creatures, **it's** ~~a~~ **doubtful** that owls are as wise as they are shown in cartoons**.**
3. good
4. Owls rely **mostly** on their sense of hearing at night, **but** they also have good vision.
5. C
6. A

Writing Warm-up 85

1. of
2. **She** had to leave the oxen exhibit, or **she'd** be late to her **doctor's** appointment**.**
3. well
4. The musk ox was **nearly** extinct, until scientists were able to **save** it.
5. C
6. C

Writing Warm-up 86

1. on
2. **He** thought it was humorous when the goose chased his sister, but he changed his mind **when** the goose started chasing him**.**
3. good
4. Some Canada geese **fly** south for the winter, **but others** don't migrate at all.
5. D
6. C

Writing Warm-up 87

1. onto, to
2. **Mandy** was sick during her winter vacation**,** so she **couldn't** ski, sled, or ice-skate**.**
3. well
4. The doctor **taught** Joe which foods would **create** allergic reactions if eaten.
5. B
6. B

Writing Warm-up 88

1. on, of
2. **The** sisters were planning a **special** surprise **for their** mom as a **Mother's Day** gift**.**
3. good
4. At first, the picture in the craft magazine **struck** her as silly, **but** she soon discovered how **(adorable, pleasing, attractive)** it looked when finished**.**
5. A
6. C

Writing Warm-up 89

1. of, along
2. **The** miniature bike trophy decorations were very **creative.**
3. well
4. They felt proud that **they** had **spent** the holiday **feeding** the people who didn't have a home.
5. A
6. B

Writing Warm-up 90

1. to, with, to, in
2. **The students** were so excited because the day for their field trip had **finally** arrived**.**
3. well
4. They **wore their** dressiest outfits to the birthday party.
5. B
6. C

QUIZ 10

1. across, during
2. **They** were traveling to **England, France,** and **Germany,** with the choir**.**
3. good, well, good, well
4. Sam wanted to **drive** instead of fly, **because** he was afraid of heights.
5. Possible answers include: intelligent, large, attractive, difficult
6. B

Writing Warm-up 91

1. nouns: money, adult
   verbs: learn, save, will, know, save
2. **She couldn't** decide **whether** to **exercise** at the gym **or** use the treadmill in her house**.**
3. bad
4. Every year, the **(small, tiny)** town bank awarded a $50 savings bond to the **child** who saved the **most** money.
5. Possible answer: Katie was saving money for a special gift.
6. A

Writing Warm-up 92

1. nouns: people, dictionaries, age, words
   adjectives: some, young
2. **She** was proud of her book **summary,** because she had worked hard**.**
3. badly
4. If you **want to** be **(an excellent, a successful)** doctor someday, then you should start preparing now.
5. Possible answer: Teachers like their students to work together.
6. B

Writing Warm-up 93

1. verbs: see, lose, will, see, follow
   conjunction: then
2. **Jack** was upset because he **heard** kids teasing him**.**
3. bad
4. The movie showed what happened when the main character got **(angry, frustrated, irate)** with his **(loving, kind, caring)** grandparents.
5. Possible answer: Joe was running late for the car show.
6. D

Writing Warm-up 94

1. adjectives: her, favorite, television
   nouns: show, man, people's, wishes
2. **Sarah** was **having** a bad day**,** but she **knew** tomorrow **would** be better**.**
3. bad
4. The simple act of smiling at someone **walking** by can brighten that person's day.
5. Possible answer: The lion was trapped and needed help.
6. D

Writing Warm-up 95

1. nouns: facts, life, facts, ways
   verbs: knowing, does, help, succeed, know, use
2. **She didn't know** how to begin her story, because her ideas were hard to

127

explain.

3. badly
4. Many successful inventors **think** of new ways to use **(items, materials)** to make life easier.
5. Possible answer: Emily has many creative ideas.
6. C

Writing Warm-up 96

1. proper noun: David
   conjunction: because
2. **It's** true that many jobs are difficult, so you must be prepared to work hard.
3. fewer
4. She felt **bad**, because she had been drawing instead of working.
5. Possible answer: Play is important for children.
6. B

Writing Warm-up 97

1. verbs: was hoping, would learn, treat
   adverbs: quietly, kindly
2. **The preparation** for the musical was going well until **John** tripped **and** fell.
3. fewer
4. The **worst student** in class was always **getting** other people in trouble.
5. Possible answer: Sue always put Margo first.
6. A

Writing Warm-up 98

1. adjective: learning
   verbs: remember, is, causes, stretch
2. **Sometimes** a **person's** best thinking takes place in **silence.**
3. fewer, fewer
4. Successful people overcame many challenges before **becoming** who they **are** today.
5. Possible answer: Rosa Parks was an important woman in history.
6. B

Writing Warm-up 99

1. nouns: countries, world, equality, citizen
   prepositions: of, to, for
2. **She** needed to go back to **school,** but she **didn't** have enough money to **buy supplies.**
3. less
4. An agreement **among** all three countries will help save the river.
5. Possible answer: There are many different worldwide causes.
6. D

QUIZ 11

1. (left to right then next line) pronoun, adverb, verb, noun, conjunction, preposition
2. **Mandy didn't know** what to get her mom for her birthday, so she made her a card.
3. fewer, less, bad, badly
4. If you have unused **(items, things)** in your home, you can **donate** them to a charity.
5. Possible answer: The math conference is next week.
6. B